Testimonials for
SIX STEPS SIX FIGURES

Writing Mentor Services

Thank you, Lauri Williams, for enabling me to recognize the talent and skills that God has placed on my life. Ever since I received Jesus Christ as my Lord and Savior, I have honestly desired to make His truths known to others, and because God sent you as my entrepreneur coach and writing mentor, I was able to write and publish my first Christian book, *Life's Lessons from the Master's Table*. It is because of your inspiration that I have become confident to begin writing the second edition of my book.

Again, thank you, Lauri. You are truly a blessing from God.

—Dorothy Gilliam, DRE, Shreveport, Louisiana

Business Coaching Services

Thank you, Lauri Williams. You have been a huge asset and inspiration to me, and your published book entitled, *Six Steps Six Figures: A Power-Packed Guide for Your Career Goals and Life God's Way*.

After reading your book and applying your principles, it empowered me to revisit my career goals. As a result of your professional services and your effective principles, I have been interviewed on the radio about my business and my book. You are, indeed, a professional woman of God who not only encouraged me to be on the radio show, but you also went the extra mile—you went with me. That impressed me!

Lauri, you are an excellent leader and mentor. I look forward to our collaboration on my projects in the future. I recommend Lauri's services to any new author or entrepreneur with a business idea who may need leadership. She will get them to their next level in life.

—NEDRA R. ALLEN, EdD
Author of From Cope to Hope:
My Life, My Struggle, God's Way
Executive Director of Omega Educational Technology Solutions, LLC

SIX STEPS
SIX FIGURES

MASTER YOUR MOVE; MIND YOUR OWN BUSINESS

SIX STEPS SIX FIGURES

A POWER-PACKED GUIDE FOR YOUR CAREER GOALS & LIFE GOD'S WAY

2nd Edition Updated & Expanded

LAURI WILLIAMS, CIEC, MCD, CEIP, Lay Chaplain

Copyrighted Material

Six Steps Six Figures: A Power-Packed Guide
for Your Career Goals & Life God's Way

Copyright © 2020 by Lauri J. Williams, Always Making Your Mark L.L.C.
All rights reserved by the author.

No part of this book may be used or reproduced in any manner whatsoever without the express written permission of Lauri Williams except in the case of brief quotations embodied in critical articles and reviews.

For information about this title or to order other books
and/or electronic media, contact the publisher:

Lauri Williams CIEC, MCD, CEIP, Lay Chaplain
P.O. Box 94797, North Little Rock, AR 72109
www.amymbizcoach.com
lauri@amymbizcoach.com

ISBNs:
978-1-7351853-0-9 (hardcover)
978-1-7351853-1-6 (softcover)
978-1-7351853-2-3 (eBook)

Printed in the United States of America

Unless otherwise indicated, Scripture quotations
from the King James Version (KJV)

CONTENTS

Preface xi
Acknowledgments xiii
Introduction to the Updated Edition xv

PART 1: SUCCESS AWAITS YOU 1

Step I — Vision 3

Step II — Networking 23

Step III — Your Marketing Tool—the Resume 35

Step IV — Getting Noticed 65

Step V — Put Your Best Foot Forward 77

Step VI — Securing the Deal 107

PART 2: MASTER YOUR MOVE; MIND YOUR OWN BUSINESS . 117

Step VII — Master Your Move—Mind Your Own Business . 119

    Use Your Tools to Become An Expert 123

    Explore "P" Attitudes of the Business World 130

    Three "C" Attitudes of Business 131

PART 3: SIX STEPS SIX FIGURES—A POWER-PACKED GUIDE FOR YOUR CAREER GOALS AND LIFE GOD'S WAY . . **139**

Step VIII — Mastering Your Move **141**

    FAME Principle #1 Focus **143**

    FAME Principle #2 Affirm **150**

    FAME Principle #3 Meditate **153**

    FAME Principle #4 Expect **155**

Appendix **161**

About the Author **165**

PREFACE

Motivational Message from the Author

I hope to inspire you to read this volume with zeal and apply the principles from this book to pursue your purpose and attain success in your career goals, business, and life.

Knowledge is the chief aim, but unless you apply knowledge, it serves no one. Read, understand, go forth, and apply the information you obtain so you can position yourself to reach the high places to which you aspire.

This power-packed guide gives advice and practical tips that others who are just like you have used to land the job of their dreams. Others have embraced courage, commitment, and confidence and launched their own successful enterprises.

Choose to leave a legacy; reach your goals and shatter the glass ceiling that has held you back for so long. You are no different from people who have achieved their dreams, no matter what your background is. Success was their destiny, and it is yours too.

Following these principles can help you attain a rewarding career or succeed in being your own boss. By staying committed to your dreams, and with much determination and persistence, you can take control of your career and your life. Your destiny starts with you.

ACKNOWLEDGMENTS

To my family, my spiritual mentors in the ministry, my fellow lay chaplains and workers in the ministry, and friends who supported and encouraged me to write this book. I would like to thank everyone for their support.

Natisha Turner, (natishadt@aol.com), thank you for your work on the design of the book's initial cover and the prior creative illustrations you created.

A special thanks to my editors at Graham Communications for their editing and support. I really enjoyed working with you from beginning to end. I have relished the professionalism and expertise.

George Foster, thank you for your inspiration and creativity in designing the cover for this second edition; you created a stunning work of art for my book. You are, indeed, talented in what you do.

Overall, thanks everyone who has helped this book come to fruition.

INTRODUCTION
to the Updated Edition

Six Steps Six Figures: *A Power-Packed Guide for Your Career Goals and Life God's Way* was originally published in 2008. It pleases me to tell you that I still receive countless demands for my expert comments, observations, and recommendations on career goals and godly perspectives as it relates to entrepreneurial topics as well.

Years have gone by, but this volume is not forgotten; it has been so instrumental in many people's lives that I've had countless requests to create another edition and incorporate perspectives on achieving success in one's own business based on the principles of this book.

In addition to the six steps highlighted in the first edition, I have provided an additional piece to solidify the six steps attained. I also present opportunities for leveraging the talents and skills you honed working for someone else and launching your own enterprise—making them work for you.

I have received praise and scores of testimonials from people whose careers I helped advance or businesses I helped launch. After reading my book, receiving my coaching services, and applying my effective principles, my clients achieved success in their careers and businesses.

Some have expressed that they discovered their purpose and gained a sense of peace as they employed or made their talents and skills work for them while providing service to others.

My chief aim is to enlighten and help others succeed in their career goals, business, and life. My philosophy is "My success brings you success." My goal each day is to operate from a place of success and walk the path my Creator intended for living my life to the fullest.

I believe this book will benefit you whether you want to build a career working for someone else or start a business of your own. When you read and absorb the nuggets offered in this book and put the knowledge gained to the test, others will see the results, you will share your experience and expertise, and thus create a chain reaction of success.

I encourage you to believe in yourself and adopt the "Three 'C' Attitudes" and try other recommendations presented in Part 2 of this volume. You will discover how being courageous, committed, and confident can help you create the best possible life.

PART 1:

Success Awaits You

STEP I—VISION

What you think is what you get.

"For as he thinketh in his heart so is he."
—Proverbs 23: 7 KJV

Are your career prospects like a disposable camera? The kind you squint through a tiny viewfinder only to see a distorted subject. You might get a good shot, but you can't see very far, and anything outside your field of vision might as well be on another planet.

Now think of a professional photographer who has a collection of lenses he carries in his bag, changing them for each unique shot. Some are telephoto lenses that capture subjects far away, while others are macro lenses enabling him to photograph a tiny, nearby flower in glorious detail. Wide-angle lenses open his perspective and frame the big picture. When you think about your life and career, don't you want to be like a photographer—able to choose the way you see your path?

No matter what your perspective is, you can change the way you see the world right now, if you're willing to change your lens. How do you do that? How do you transform your views, possess a new level of thinking, and take action?

This book is about creating better opportunities for yourself and open to the many ways your Creator has mapped out for you. In other words, creating a resume for your life. How do you make your life resume relevant? Create a vision with a clear objective and commit to it, just like the one featured on your professional resume. While the objective is an important part of any winning job resume, it's the most important part for your life resume, because it defines what you want to do and be. Focus on your preferred job position or career. Create a clear picture in your mind for the job you want that will enable you to prosper.

> "Commit thou way to the Lord; trust also in Him; and He shall bring it to pass."
> ~ Psalm 37:5 KJV

That kind of success requires a new level of thinking and a new perspective. If you succeed—and this book will make that possible—you will be empowered to change your limiting beliefs. You will be able to create powerful new beliefs that build and uplift you—beliefs that propel you to your destiny!

Years ago, I went through a very emotionally and financially challenging career phase. I had been working hard for the wrong reasons, and I wasn't happy. I realized I was climbing the wrong career ladder of success because I felt no passion or drive or sense of direction for it. Once I acknowledged my feelings, I was able to set the right career goals. I began to seek out training that sharpened my skills in coaching, mentoring, advising, and consulting with clients; the services I provided gave me passion and a sense of fulfillment as I launched out to help others achieve their career goals and purpose for their careers and personal life. Months later, I established my company, OPTASIA Career and Training Services (Now called: Always Making Your Mark LLC) I had chosen the name OPTASIA, which means vision in Hebrew, because I wanted to help clients achieve their desired career and life goals.

How can you improve your vision? Here are two simple but powerful techniques. The first is: **change your lens**. If you look through a distorted lens, you will see a distorted picture. For instance, speaking negatively about yourself and focusing on certain limiting beliefs will produce a habit of seeing yourself in a negative light. So, don't go down that road.

Saying daily affirmations is one of the most important steps to improving your life. Affirmations are positive, uplifting statements about yourself that you repeat to yourself—almost like an uplifting mantra. When you repeat positive affirmations, you are firmly imprinting these ideas into your subconscious mind or your spiritual inner man. Some examples are:

1. "Each day I am getting stronger and I am getting better and better" (Proverbs 31:25, KJV).

2. "I shall flourish in life; wealth, wisdom, and riches dwell in my house" (Psalm 112:3, KJV).

3. "I shall not yield to defeat; I always triumph over my circumstances" (2 Corinthians 2:14, KJV).

4. "I am out of debt. My needs are met; I have plenty more to put in store" (Philippians 4:19, KJV).

Say these statements (or create your own) for five or ten minutes daily, intently focusing your attention on your affirmations, much like you learned multiplication tables as a child. Repeat your affirmation for 40 days, and you will notice your life begin to change. I find this devotional exercise encouraging to me because I know that my words are not just my words, but my Creator's words.

The philosopher René Descartes famously said, "I think, therefore I am." We now know that, what you think, you will become.

Keep a journal of this experience that includes "before" and "after" notes. The "before" notes will remind you how you felt and your self-defeating thoughts before you embarked upon your affirmation quest. The "after" notes will show you the emotional changes that occur as you practice the affirmation method. You also can journal about your new attitude and the life-changing events as a result of these affirmations.

Individual results may vary. Don't be discouraged if your thought patterns don't immediately change. As with a seed, it takes time to grow. Be patient. Nurture your mind. Feed it positive, productive words and thoughts; thus, wait for the harvest. As you practice the affirmation technique, you will notice that it becomes easier.

Consistently affirm yourself until uplifting ideas are imprinted in your mind, until thinking and speaking positively about yourself are as much a part of your daily routine as eating, drinking, or brushing your teeth.

> "Drive thy business or thy business will drive thee."
> ~ Benjamin Franklin

The second technique is: **focus on your target.** A photographer focuses on his subject through the viewfinder while tuning out the distractions around him. In our daily lives, we focus—or hold thoughts in our head without attending to other matters—every day, even if we aren't aware that we are doing it. What do you focus on? Are you focusing on your past, the events and failures already behind you that you cannot change? Are you focusing on the things happening around you that are of little importance? Either way, you'll never see a clear picture of what's possible. In fact, you'll miss the beautiful scene in front of you. Instead of focusing on the past and trivial things, concentrate on the positive things you want (Philippians 3:14 KJV). See yourself succeeding. Focus on your future today. Start right now!

Have you ever used a camera with an auto-focus? At first when you point your camera at your subject, you see a blurry image. Press the button halfway down, and suddenly everything comes into focus. You must do that with your life. How? By creating an action plan that enables you to achieve the professional life you've always dreamed with just a few steps (Proverbs 16:3 KJV):

1. Research careers that have always intrigued you and their respective salary ranges. Also, look into or investigate the stress levels of the positions you're targeting and make sure the stress levels align with what you're looking for.

2. Interview people you know who are currently working in the field or position you're interested in (Psalm 37:37, KJV).

3. Develop your own position description by surfing job sites and collecting job announcements. This will give you a sense of what employers are looking for.

Building Blocks of Success

Activity Worksheet

It's never too early or too late to change your life. By reviewing the Building Block Activity Sheet (See figure 1-A), we can aspire to greatness in whatever endeavors we choose, whether it be pursuing a rewarding career or choosing to own or launch a business. The objective of this exercise is to provoke desire and inspire you to achieve your best in whatever you do. Remember, if you think you can, you can, but if you don't try, you will never know if you could.

Let's look at these columns that highlight some well-known people (**now you can choose to observe others you prefer that have made successful paths in their life journey, but I have listed ones that came to mind**) who have achieved fame and success in reaching their career goals:

Bill Gates surpassed the millionaire status in the second column (ages 16–30). In fact, he made billions as a young man. He was a Harvard dropout with a vision and determination. You, too, can succeed with the right mindset and willingness.

Oprah Winfrey made her first million in the mid-1980s in the third column (ages 31–45). Billionaire and philanthropist Warren Buffett belongs in this column as well.

Harland Sanders, also known as Colonel Sanders, made millions in column five (ages 61–75) from 600 franchised Kentucky Fried Chicken outlets. In 1960, he sold his interest in the company for $2 million (that's over $7 million today) to a group of investors.

See if you can place any famous or wealthy people you're familiar with in these columns. The idea is not to get depressed if you feel life is slipping by, but to mark your progress and set your course. Your success is dependent upon your will, not your age, but there is no better time to get started than today.

My business never would have been created had I approached it with cold, unfeeling logic. I had to believe in what I was doing just like Bill Gates, Oprah Winfrey, Warren Buffett, and Col. Sanders. Set your goals and achieve them by becoming passionate about them. Enlist your emotions and your senses as you envision your goals. Breathe life into those goals. Be productive. Make success so real that you can touch it, smell it, and taste it, and you'll get there faster.

Building Blocks of Success
ACTIVITY WORKSHEET

Figure 1-A

COLUMN 1	COLUMN 2	COLUMN 3	COLUMN 4	COLUMN 5	COLUMN 6
AGES 1–15	AGES 16–30	AGES 31–45	AGES 46–60	AGES 61–75	AGES 76–90
1	16	31	46	61	76
2	17	32	47	62	77
3	18	33	48	63	78
4	19	34	49	64	79
5	20	35	50	65	80
6	21	36	51	66	81
7	22	37	52	67	82
8	23	38	53	68	83
9	24	39	54	69	84
10	25	40	55	70	85
11	26	41	56	71	86
12	27	42	57	72	87
13	28	43	58	73	88
14	29	44	59	74	89
15	30	45	60	75	90

Who Is Responsible for Y.O.U.?

Every day offers an opportunity for improvement, but only you are responsible for your personal development. Self-improvement begins with you, so use every moment to advance the pursuit of your goals. To learn this concept, one of your daily affirmations could be, "Each day I am getting better and better." Another affirmation might be "One more day closer to launching my empire." If you have a passion for writing and desire to publish a book, I suggest this affirmation: "I am now writing my best-selling book."

Goal Setting

Imagine planning a trip without a destination in mind. You wash and gas up the car, pack your bags, fasten your seatbelts, and turn on the ignition. Before shifting out of park, you stomp on the gas a couple of times just to hear the satisfying roar of the engine. And then you just stare out the windshield at the garage wall without a clue what to do next. Why? Because you never had a destination in mind; you never had a goal. So, a goal is basically a plan with steps to take action to achieve.

Both life and your job search are like this. If you don't know where you want to go, you'll never go anywhere, or you'll end up in the wrong place (Hosea 4:6, KJV). Where do you want to go? Only you can answer that question.

Now imagine a trip with a destination. You know where you are going; you have set a goal. And you have that same car, all gassed up, washed, and ready to go. But then you start to question: Will my car really make it that far? What if I get carsick along the way? What if my gas gauge malfunctions? Maybe I'd be better off just sitting here in the driveway or going back inside and skipping the journey altogether.

It's one thing to know where you want to go. It's another to believe you can actually get there (Mark 9:23, KJV). When you set goals, you must begin by inspecting your mind to see what viewpoints and thought processes prevent you from having the job of your dreams or the success that you desire. If you discover areas that inhibit you, then you must make a plan of action and transform them.

Before you begin your job search, establish clear goals that define your objectives and express what you want to accomplish. Ask yourself the following questions:

1. What can I do this year to prepare myself for finding the right job?

2. What additional knowledge or skills would I like to attain to become more marketable?

3. What do I need to possess in order to achieve my job search goal?

4. How can others (i.e., family, friends, and colleagues) help me?

5. How can I maximize my employer search to target the right company for me?

You can also consider asking yourself similar questions pertaining to starting your own business:

1. What can I do this year to prepare myself for starting my own business?

2. What additional knowledge, training, or licenses would I need to attain to attract the right clientele and make my business stand out from my competitors?

3. How can I secure funding to help me launch my enterprise?

Tips for Setting Your Job Search or Entrepreneurial Goals

1. Write specific, measurable, attainable, realistic, and timely (S.M.A.R.T) goals on a piece of paper or in a document on your computer.

2. Make sure the goals are clear and specific, not vague generalities. If you have several goals, prioritize them.

> "If thy faint in the day of adversity; thy strength is small:
> ~ **Proverbs 24:10 KJV**

3. Include dates and time frames.

4. Make positive statements.

Step I—Vision

Specific = _____ You Must Answer Six Questions (What, When, Where, Why, Who, and How)
- What job or venture do I want to pursue?
- When do I want to achieve it?
- Where would I like to work or operate a business?
- Why do I feel this job is the right fit for me?
- Who can help me achieve this goal?
- How can I get funding for that venture?

Measurable = _____

Attainable = _____

Realistic = _____

Timely = _____

Use the sample goal form (See figure 1-B) to help you define and achieve each of your goals. Use one page for each goal.

Sample Goal Form

Figure 1-B

Write down one or two goals you would like to achieve in the next week or month. Be specific.

Goal 1: _____
_____

Goal 2: _____
_____

List two actions you will take to attain these goals. Be as specific as possible. Also, you must include a time frame.

Action 1: _____
_____

Action 2: _____
_____

Pinpoint possible barriers to attaining these goals. Be specific.

Barrier 1: _____
_____

Barrier 2: _____
_____

Describe the action(s) you will take to overcome these barriers. Be specific.

Action 1: _____
_____

Action 2: _____
_____

Evaluate your success in attaining these goals.

_____
_____
_____

You have likely seen transportation companies with messages on large trucks saying, "How is my driving?" The questions are asked to gauge or measure the effectiveness of their transportation line of business. Likewise, treat your career goals or entrepreneurial quest the same way. Evaluate your efforts and see what steps worked in landing you an interview or securing funding for your start-up and be persistent.

Job Search Planning Checklists

Job searching requires effective planning. Major companies are hiring every day, but you must have a clear vision and an effective plan of action to attain the job or career of your dreams. Decide today that you will no longer let opportunity slip by you. Make a commitment to yourself to proactively plan and be available when opportunities arise.

Here are three planning tools that can help bring to the surface the subtle questions or concerns associated with planning your job search:

Self-Assessment Checklist
- ✓ I have two or three firm choices of careers I plan to pursue.
- ✓ I have created a list of jobs I am interested in pursuing.
- ✓ I have identified personal strengths, skills, and interests.

Desired Work Situation Checklist
- ✓ I have researched organizations or companies that might hire someone with my skills, interests, and background.
- ✓ I have identified geographic areas where I would be willing to relocate.
- ✓ I have identified 5 potential employers with whom I want to work.
- ✓ I have researched career-field, entry-level jobs with salaries and best geographic locations.

Ready and Available Checklist
- ✓ I have an appropriate wardrobe for interviews.
- ✓ I have practiced and honed my interviewing skills.

- ✓ I have a professional-sounding voicemail message in case an employer calls.
- ✓ I have three professional contacts who will serve as references.
- ✓ I have prepared a portfolio to highlight my experience, skills, and talents.

Self-Assessment

- ✓ Career plans
- ✓ Job interests
- ✓ Personal skills and strengths

Desired Work Situation

- ✓ Companies and compatibility factors
- ✓ Relocation issues
- ✓ Employer details
- ✓ Career fields and salary factors

Ready and Available

- ✓ Appropriate attire for interviews
- ✓ Interviewing skills
- ✓ Professional point of contact
- ✓ References
- ✓ Prepared portfolio

Checklist for Entrepreneurs

There are many elements for succeeding in business. Having an effective guide or checklist can most certainly help you stay focused. See a few sample items in the checklist below that you may want to consider as you pursue your entrepreneurial venture. Prerequisites are discussed in further detail later in this book.

Self-Assessment Checklist for Entrepreneurs

- ✓ I have identified my personal goals for starting a business.
- ✓ I have considered one or two areas of business I would like to pursue.
- ✓ I have identified my knowledge, talents, skills, passion, and strengths for the type of business I want to run.
- ✓ I have tested and promoted my product or service and determined there are enough customers for competition.

Information Resource Checklist for Entrepreneurs

- ✓ I have identified geographic areas where I would be willing to set up and run my business. Location is an important factor.
- ✓ I have researched ways to find experts or prospective mentors in associations that can assist me in learning more about my industry or field and target market.
- ✓ I have identified possible competition and analyzed pricing strategies for competition.

Ready and Available Checklist for Entrepreneurs
- ✓ I have clarified my business's mission, objectives, and goals.
- ✓ I network effectively; I can deliver an effective elevator pitch of products or services.
- ✓ I have identified possible competition and analyzed strategies for driving customers to my website or place of business.

STEP II—NETWORKING

Insider Tips

"A man's gift maketh room for him, and bringeth him before great men."
—Proverbs 18:16 KJV

Finding the ideal job or career can seem frustrating and a bit overwhelming. That's why you can't do it alone. Thankfully, you don't have to.

Unless you live on a deserted island or prefer to be a hermit, you have a personal network. A network is an interconnected group of people or resources. Your network is comprised of your connections to other people, and it is the key to your success. The members of your network possess a wealth of information—more than you could ever know—and their networks include people who can help you achieve your dreams if you add them to yours (Proverbs 27:17, KJV).

How do you network? This question has danced in the minds of many. The answer is: there are many ways. In fact, this book cannot include every strategy for connecting with people who can play a part in fulfilling your destiny. But I can recommend three steps that will help you start.

These steps are:

1. Take inventory by determining who you already know and how they can help.

2. Learn the tricks of the trade to expand your network outside your comfort zone.

3. Armed with this knowledge, put yourself in places where you can succeed.

First, take inventory. Who do you know?
The hiring process at most companies involves extensive planning. In fact, it can be months between the time an employee announces he is leaving and the time that position is open to you. Meanwhile, employers look to their employees to fill that job. To compete with them, you need inside information, and the people you know are often the best source. Whether you're looking for a home, car, business opportunity, or a job, the best deals are first revealed to insiders—employees, family members, friends, professional acquaintances, and finally strangers.

Importantly, it is good to know that professional networks like LinkedIn are a good resource for jump-starting your networking campaign. LinkedIn can be effective for finding jobs and other professional opportunities while staying in touch with coworkers and acquaintances. I like LinkedIn because it is a useful tool that can help you stay in touch with your contacts and allows you to share ideas and build your professional career. So, don't be a stranger when it comes to your career! The larger your pool of friendly contacts, the better your chances of finding a golden opportunity—your ideal job.

Thankfully, you already have a larger network than you realize, but it helps to understand how to categorize your relationships. I've listed two types of networks: professional and personal, and, of course, people can be categorized as both.

Professional networks are an advantage to you as you climb the career ladder. Members of your professional network include managers, past and present; coworkers, past and present; fellow members of professional associations; and fellow members of college alumni associations. These last two associations can be particularly helpful. If you are not a member of a professional association, join one right away. It will give you a chance to network with others who have similar interests. Your membership and active participation will give you inside information, and you'll have opportunities to participate in training programs that increase your marketability for your desired job. Surf the web, looking for local professional associations. A good place to start is the current publication of the *Encyclopedia of Associations*.

Personal networks are just as important. They include family, friends, fellow civic and social club members, and members of your church or house of worship. You should become involved in your community if you aren't already. It keeps you informed about local events and helps you establish your own community network bank.

Keep in mind that establishing these networks purely for personal gain won't benefit you very much. Instead, seek to make a positive impact on others' lives, and eventually it will come back to you. Help others fulfill their dreams, and they'll help you fulfill yours. Plus, if you show an interest in others, you'll learn about their careers and employers, and eventually you'll be able to ask for information to help you advance your career.

Second, know the tricks of the trade.
Your networking approach depends largely on your relationships with others and their relevance to you. Your strategy depends on your personality, interests, responsibilities, and other facets of your life. But, regardless of who you are, you need a networking action plan in which you outline your networking goals and the steps you will take to reach those goals. While each person's plan is different, they all include an aggressive networking method, where you strategically set a goal for the number of new contacts you want to make each hour, day, or week. To illustrate: say you decide to make 8 new contacts per day, which equals 1 contact per hour, totaling 40 new people in your network each week who can help you achieve your goals.

The key to successful networking is not simply to meet as many people as possible but to leave a lasting impression on those who can help you achieve a six-figure (and beyond) income or another worthy goal. Ralph Waldo Emerson said it best, "Don't go where the path may lead. Instead, go where there is no path and leave a trail." The people who can help you achieve your goals interact with so many people daily, they can't possibly remember everyone; therefore, you must blaze a trail, so you remain on their mind even when you are not with them.

How do you blaze a trail? It depends on you. I can teach you how to network, but blazing that network trail will depend on you incorporating strategies that work best for you. You must write your own book through trial and error. You will have successes and failures; the key is to learn the right lessons, so you can maximize success and minimize failure. According to a wise proverb: "Wisdom is a principle thing and in all your getting, get an understanding" (Proverbs 4:7, KJV). This holds true in knowing how you effectively network with people.

You should establish a plan for remembering key people that will propel you to your destiny. An effective recommendation is to take advantage of technological tools. An approach I suggest is to consider using Excel, especially if you are skilled with this program. It can be very beneficial when storing an extensive amount of data such as names and addresses.

Indeed, understanding the importance of remembering your networks and making it personal can have added value. Know that if you are equipped with this knowledge, you have taken a major step closer to your goal. If you are not equipped with this knowledge, or if you do not apply it, your network will not help you any more than it is now, and it may help you less.

Remembering key people starts with learning their names (Proverbs 22:1, KJV). Nothing solidifies a new relationship like the ability to recall a person's name and use it confidently in a greeting. Meanwhile, forgetting a person's name can stop a relationship dead in its tracks. Few social encounters are more awkward than when one-half of your brain is focused on a conversation with an acquaintance while the other desperately flips through your mental address book trying to remember their name. This person who could have helped you achieve your goals leaves the interaction wondering why you seemed so distracted or, worse, realizes what happened.

Two powerful yet simple strategies that many of my clients have found helpful are using acronyms and keywords. Acronyms are words formed from the first letters of other words, such as NASA, which stands for National Aeronautics and Space Administration. Creating acronyms is a simple way to help you jog your memory. Think back to your childhood when your teacher taught you this strategy before a big exam. What are the colors of the rainbow? Why, ROYGBIV: red, orange, yellow, green, blue, indigo, and violet, of course! My children used this strategy when they studied for their tests.

You can apply this strategy when meeting people as well. Want to remember the name of Paul Arnold in public affairs? Use "PAPA" until you know him well enough that you don't need this memory device. If you can't create an acronym that sounds like a real word, make up a word instead. In fact, silly-sounding acronyms are often easier to remember than common ones.

The image-naming keyword method is another effective way to remember the names of new contacts. This is when you create a relationship between a person's name and their physical characteristics. For instance, say I meet a person name Gregg Washington who works at Washington Mutual Corporation. I notice he has features like George Washington on the dollar bill. When I hear about Washington Mutual Corporation or see a dollar bill, it will trigger me to remember Gregg Washington. This helps to keep him fresh in my mind.

You don't have to use only one strategy to help you remember names. A friend of mine recently joined a church with several hundred people, and he discovered that, after several weeks, he could remember peoples' faces but no names. This frustrated him, so he stuck a sheet of paper in his Bible and made a point of asking people's names, reading name tags, and listening for names in conversations. Then he wrote their names on the sheet of paper along with a few things he had learned about them and perhaps a distinguishing feature, such as "kind-looking, balding, older gentleman" or "resembles Cindy." Each Sunday before church, he made a point of studying that sheet, and as it grew longer, he could greet more people by name.

Third, put yourself in places where you can succeed. Finding the right job lead means being ready to look in the right places. Since you never know who you are going to meet and when you may meet them, it is important that you maintain a professional appearance and keep an inventory of business cards. Treat every contact as if it were an interview. This helps you gather information you may need in the future.

There are certain circumstances, such as training conferences and job fairs, that are tailor-made for networking. Be proactive when attending job training seminars and conferences, because the associates you meet may have knowledge about upcoming job openings and promotions. Also, participate in job fairs. Some online resources for promoting job fairs or providing job search information are: www.indeed.com; www.clearancejobs.com; www.aarp.org; www.abilitylinks.org. Job fair information is listed in your newspaper or are often scheduled at colleges and universities. Remember, at job fairs, prospective employers are looking for you as much as you are looking for them. Learn about their culture, mission, and structure so you can decide if you want to work for them. And to ensure success, follow the Boy Scout motto: "Be prepared." Bring an updated resume that is easy to read—one or two pages in length—and applicable to two or three specific jobs (You might want to bring more than one type of resume, in fact). Write a script for what you want to say to employers and practice it. When you arrive, be friendly and speak clearly.

Don't wait for people or opportunities to seek you out. Instead, pursue your own destiny by never letting a good opportunity pass you by. The world is made up of two kinds of people: possibility thinkers and impossibility thinkers. Impossibility thinkers make excuses for why they can't network.

They fear rejection, or they tell themselves and others, "I am not a brown-noser." What rubbish! No man is an island, and we need each other to help us succeed in life. Instead, be a possibility thinker. Possibility thinkers pursue opportunities to network and enjoy the fruits of their networking. They aren't afraid of rejection, because they know that "no" often simply means, "Not at this time." I try to instill in my clients: "He who tooteth not his own horn, it gets not tooteth." If you are good at something, tell people. You know your talents and skills far better than anyone else does, so no one can sell your unique product—you—like you can.

John's Networking Success

I remember listening to a person quote a passage from Max Gunther's book, *The Luck Factor*. He mentioned that Gunther attested that the most lucrative job offers come from acquaintances. One of my clients, who I'll call "John," would certainly agree. He managed to land a six-figure salary by applying the networking action plan and the aggressive networking method.

Here's how John tells his story: "I was working for the federal government traveling around the world, and I wanted a change. I wanted a change in my work environment and an increase in my income. I started searching through classified ads and various internet websites, but nothing seemed to be the right fit for me. The jobs that I liked were already filled by someone else. That is when I came to Lauri Williams and learned more about the benefits of networking. I gathered the information taught and modified the networking action plan to accommodate my career interests. I followed the plan to purposely network with a minimum of 20 people per week. It seemed overwhelming at first, but when I organized the contacts daily, it was a piece of cake. Meeting four new people a day was not difficult because I would meet lots of people while traveling.

"As I continued to employ my networking action plan, my contact list grew immensely, and I was prepared because I learned name association and other networking strategies (acronyms and keywords, etc.), which helped me to remember names. Using acronyms to memorize groups of names was simple for me because I had become familiar with the concept while working for the government. One example: I met a professional contact named Bob Arnold from Pittsburgh, Pennsylvania, (BAPP). That is just one of many networking tips that help me to organize my networking contact database without forgetting people."

> "It's not just what you know or who you know, but it's who knows what you know."
> ~ Author unknown

When John mentioned that he had a networking database, I asked him how he distinguished his contacts. John simply said, "I have a green networking business card binder, which represents money and the people who can influence in my career. I follow up with these contacts every 30 days to keep my name fresh in their minds."

He also mentioned that he had a red networking business card binder for those he was not sure would benefit him professionally. He would follow up with these contacts every 45–60 days, so they could get to know each other. It was one of these contacts that helped John land his six-figure income. That's right—his life-changing opportunity came from his red binder, not the green one. You never know who will help you achieve your goals. It pays to network.

STEP III—YOUR MARKETING TOOL—THE RESUME

Marketing and YOU

"Commit thy works unto the Lord, and thy thoughts shall be established."

—Proverbs 16:3 KJV

Job searching can be a painless process if tackled with knowledge, confidence, and the right tools. One of the most important tools is your resume.

When you are going through your job search process, you are marketing yourself in the same way a real estate agent tries to sell a house: You are finding a need and then filling it. Your customer is your potential employer, and your products are your skills and experience. Like the advertising circulars you receive in the mail from your real estate agent, your resume is a marketing piece that advertises you and gives you a chance to close the sale in an interview.

Think about how you sort through your mail. Every day when I come home, I go through the stack. Bills go in a special place to be read and dealt with all at once. I read personal letters and notes immediately. And the advertising circulars? They had better catch my eye and fill a need, or I toss them.

The human resources specialist at your prospective employer opens scores of emails. He or she doesn't have time to carefully read lengthy resumes for each job opening, so anything that doesn't match job advertisement or catch their eye of prospective openings or meet their company's need could be eliminated from the application pile.

Figure 3-A (below) is a marketing model that illustrates how the marketing process can apply to your job search endeavors. Notice the similarities between your job search and the process that marketers use to find consumers like you.

Figure 3-A: Job Search Marketing Model (JSMM)

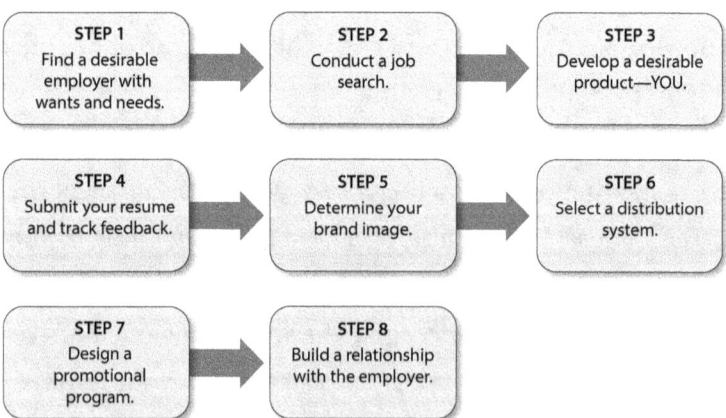

The first step in the job search process is to find a desirable employer with a need, much like a company focuses its resources on likely buyers. This is the reason you see beer and pickup trucks advertised during football games instead of classical music CDs and laundry detergent. To do this, you search classifieds and the internet, contact employment agencies, and network with family, friends, and professional contacts. An excellent networking resource is LinkedIn.

You then develop a way to package your desirable product—you—by submitting your resume to employers in various industries where you are willing to work. Keep a record of the responses and continue to update your resume and skills as often as possible. You should associate this process with creating your brand image in the same way that companies want you to associate their products with certain characteristics. In other words, you must demonstrate how your skills and abilities exceed that of your competitors—the people applying for the same position that you want.

The next step in the job search marketing process is to select a distribution system. This means that you must strategically plan how to get your resume to the employer. You can choose to submit via the internet on various employers' websites, or by applying online through USAJOBS.gov and indeed.com. This is another way to have your resume delivered to the employer instead of in person. Either way, you want the customer/employer to know who you are, what you have to offer, and how you can make an impact on the organization.

Designing a promotional program as it relates to selling yourself on paper is necessary in order to motivate the potential employer to contact you for an interview. This involves what advertisers call the AIDA Model. (See Figure 3-B). The AIDA Model consists of the four steps consumers take when making a purchase: Attention, Interest, Desire, and Action. Advertisers study how consumers take these steps to influence them to buy their products and services. Since employers go through these same steps during the hiring process, you should act like an advertiser and study them, so your resume can attract their attention, pique their interest, cause them to desire your services and, finally, take action and offer you an interview and, eventually, a six-figure salary. The last step in the job search marketing process consists of building a relationship with employers, continually adapting to changes in the job market in order to meet their needs.

Figure 3-B: Attention Interest Desire and Action (AIDA MODEL)

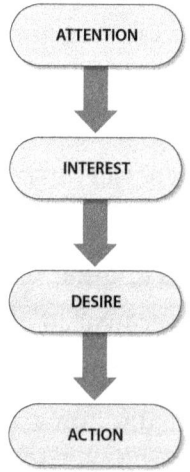

Using Your Resume Effectively

A resume introduces you to an employer; if yours isn't right, you'll be eliminated. Employers do not have time to read every resume, so your goal is to get yours noticed. Two strategies that will help you do this are personifying your resume and speaking your employer's language.

Personify Your Resume

An effective resume gets the attention of employers, but a little networking beforehand can help secure your prospects of getting it into the right hands. Personifying your resume—putting a face to the page through a personal contact—may not be easy, but if you can establish rapport through a face-to-face meeting or a brief phone call, take every opportunity to do so. This may require a little strategic planning, but if your potential employer already knows your relevant experience when they come across your resume, they will stop and read more.

The next time you find out about a job opening for which you are qualified, inquire about the hiring manager within that company. This will give you an added advantage over applicants who don't conduct this research. Remember, researching information about hiring managers and creating ways to establish rapport with them will put you ahead.

Employers' Universal Language: Numbers

As with any consumer, employers want to know the answer to one question: "What's in it for me?" Your resume must contain impact statements or accomplishments that demonstrate how you will fulfill an employer's needs. In other words, how will you help them make a profit or accomplish their mission?

Our world is comprised of many different nationalities with many different languages, but in the corporate world, everyone understands numbers. You need to speak that language. Speaking numbers tells an employer what you did and how well you did it. In other words, numbers help make it easy to see profit. And that's what most employers are looking for.

Below are a few factors employers look for when considering an applicant:

- Will the applicant help me make money?
- Will the applicant help me save money?
- Does the applicant manage time well?
- Does the applicant possess the skills for the job?
- Is the applicant a problem solver?
- Is the applicant willing to learn?
- Does the applicant build relationships with internal and external customers?
- Can the applicant contribute to our company's growth?
- Can the applicant attract new customers?
- Can the applicant help us retain existing customers?
- Is the applicant competitive (sales)?

Accomplishments Support the Universal Language of Numbers

In the upper echelons of management, especially jobs with six-figure salaries, accomplishments are one of the key factors employers look for in screening applicants. When developing your resume, you must list accomplishments that demonstrate that you have completed projects that are difficult and worthwhile, and that help you stand out among your competitors.

Here's a suggestion: The next time you receive recognition or contribute significantly to your company's goals, remember to document your actions and update your resume. Your accomplishments should be numbers-based, profit-driven, and demonstrative of corporate values. Accomplishments that are not numbers-based, profit-driven, or that don't demonstrate corporate value are ineffective. It can reduce your chances of landing an interview because it leaves room for questions. Keep this in mind when you draft your accomplishments—anything less can reduce your chances of getting an interview. Words and phrases that strengthen your list of accomplishments include the following:

- New training programs
- Improved, efficient operations
- Outstanding customer service
- Mission management
- Teamwork
- Emergency-planning
- Saved money
- Solved a problem

Below are examples of less effective and more effective accomplishments.

Less effective:
- Implemented a process change that improved downtime

More effective:
- Standardized engineering change order procedures that reduced turnaround time. Improved production 27 percent and reduced assembly-line downtime from 8 hours to 4 hours.

Less effective:
- Supported research and development in achieving goals for new products brought to market

More effective:
- As Director of Quality Assurance R&D, supported research and development in achieving a 78 percent increase in new products brought to market.

Less effective:
- Improved branch ranking for sales volume to number 1

More effective:
- As Senior Sales Branch Manager, improved sales production 50 percent and increased branch ranking status from number 12 to number 1 in a 14-branch district.

Keyword Design

When creating your resume, make sure that it contains enough and the right kinds of keywords for your industry. Keywords are words that describe your job title, skillset, knowledge base, degrees, licensures, certifications, software experience, and professional affiliations. These words are usually nouns or noun phrases; however, verbs can be used. Adding keywords increases the chance of your resume moving to the top of an employer's candidate list. One way you can ensure you have right keywords for resume is to review job announcement and incorporate keywords from there to your resume. Only incorporate the specific keywords that truly match your experience.

Occasionally, you will see a job announcement that includes preferred but not required specific qualification(s). This simply means that the employer would like for you to have the qualifications, but a lack of them is not a reason to screen you out. If an employer mentions that certain qualification(s) are required, then your resume must include them, or it will be flagged, and you will not be considered for an interview (See sample vacancy announcements).

Sample Keywords

Job/Profession/ Industry
- Sales
- Cold-calling
- Project management
- Accounts payable

Technical Terms
- Hardware
- Software

Certifications
- Microsoft Certification
- Six Sigma—Lean Certification
- Professional Human Resources (PHR) Certification

Degrees
- Master of Business Administration (MBA)
- Master of Public Administration (MPA)
- Registered Nurse (RN)
- Bachelor of Science, Nursing (BSN)

Where to Find Keywords

Keywords can be found by researching classified advertisements, newspapers, periodicals, and company websites (see sample job posting with keywords). A resource that I find helpful for accessing employer keywords is the Occupation Information Network, or O*Net, at http://online.onetcenter.org/. Try staying current with keywords. Maintain active involvement with your local industry's professional associations. Again, this is where networking pays off.

Electronic Resumes

Update your electronic resume once a month to ensure that you are using current keywords. Also, change your resume to match any new jobs that you are considering applying for online. If an employer posts a position and you see that you have the right keywords, but not the mentioned qualifications, apply anyway.

How Employers Use Keyword Searches

Employers often use keywords to distinguish job candidates who have submitted resumes online. They also pay to search job board databases for candidates, conducting searches by:

- Date resume submitted
- Past/present tense keywords
- Location (city/town) where applicant resides
- Most recent employer
- Job title
- Salary
- Experience level
- Full-time/part-time preference
- Company category

Keywords help employers determine an applicant's relevancy factor—how applicable their skills are for a job opening—and reduce the number of prospects, who at that point are just names on resumes. Here's how it works:

Keywords = sales, marketing, advertising

Jane has the words "sales," "marketing," and "advertising" in her resume, and Susan only has the word "sales." Jane's experience is more relevant.

NOTE: Be sure not to overdo it. Resumes with too many keywords are screened out.

The relevancy factor also relates to how often candidates update their resumes in an online system, so it is important that you update your electronic resume as often as possible.

Again, Jane and Susan have the same words that appear the same number of times in their resumes, but Jane updated her resume within the last month, while Susan updated hers two months ago. Jane's resume is more recent and, therefore, is more relevant.

Below are sample job announcements by employers who use keywords. Notice which words are repeated. Those are the words a prospective employee will need to include when she or he responds.

Sample Vacancy (JOB) Announcements Using Keywords

JOB ANNOUNCEMENT 1: Systems Engineer
The incumbent will act as main point of contact for **technical issues** at the **weapon-systems level** providing accurate and timely resolutions.
Main Duties: will include but not be limited to the following:
- Working closely with DOD customers to ensure a thorough understanding of requirements.
- Working closely with **Engineering and senior technical staff** on the production of estimations.

- Engaging with customers to help plan deployment strategies and implement these converting evaluations and trials to customer wins.
- **Solve** complex scientific and engineering problems, such as the **development of new transportation systems**, the **design** of rockets, or the improvement of communications systems.

Qualifications and Experience

Education/Experience
- BSCS or equivalent, plus 4–7 years of experience in middleware development, (i.e., APIs, messaging software, distributed systems, or networking software)
- Experience as a member of a multiperson software development team
- Must be able to work independently or on a team project

Required Skills:
- Experience in the deployment of network infrastructure software products
- 5+ years of experience in Sales/System engineering deploying technology-focused products in the Financial Services industry
- 5+ years of experience with middleware technology (TIBCO, IBM MQ, etc.)
- Strong knowledge of Market Data infrastructure (Feed Handlers, FIX Engines, Pricing Engines, Ticker Plants)

- Direct Market Data Feed connectivity (OPRA, NASDAQ, Inet, Arca, etc.)
- Strong Unix/Linux skills

Desirable Skills:
- Excellent listening skills to understand the business needs of prospects and existing customers
- 5+ years of experience in Sales/System engineering deploying technology-focused products in the Financial Services industry
- 5+ years of experience with middleware technology (TIBCO, IBM MQ, etc)
- Strong knowledge of Market Data infrastructure (Feed Handlers, FIX Engines, Pricing Engines, Ticker Plants)
- Experience developing applications in either C, C#, or JAVA
- Experience developing applications on pub/sub systems in the financial services industry Direct Market Data Feed connectivity (OPRA, NASDAQ, Inet, Arca, etc.)

JOB ANNOUNCEMENT 2: Marketing and Sales Account Executive:

Main Duties: The incumbent will be responsible for negotiating and selling online **advertising** to businesses in North America. Candidate must develop account opportunities, interface with editorial team to define new product offerings, work with management on sales strategy and **sell**/close product packages to meet their business goals.

Qualifications and Experience

Required Skills:
- Must be a Senior Account Executive with at least 5–10 years of online **advertising sales** experience
- Must be able to **stimulate sales** through **cold calling, telemarketing**, and networking
- Previous leadership experience is required; proven negotiation skills are a must.
- Should demonstrate exceptional customer focus and be confident communicators in phone, written, and face-to-face settings
- A minimum of five years proven direct sales experience primarily in advertising or internet sales and including sales transactions with CEO/VP-level management required
- Must have excellent sales skills to successfully bring in new business and respond to an ever-changing market, and strong relationship skills for follow-up sales and service with existing accounts
- Must be able to demonstrate strong skills in initiating high-level contacts in accounts and their agencies, acquiring sales presentation opportunities and the ability to close business

Desirable Skills:
- Ideal candidate has existing relationships with media buyers and advertising clients.

- An action-oriented, results-driven individual able to make sound and timely decisions in a fast-paced environment where product offerings and features change rapidly

Resume Formats (Choosing the Right Tool)

There is no one correct way to design a resume. Choosing the right format is simply a matter of reviewing your professional experience, accomplishments, and your skills and qualifications for the position(s) you are seeking. But whatever resume format you choose, always begin with the most relevant and impressive items. After all, it's what the employer will read first. And always make sure someone you trust reads your resume to offer helpful tips. Two heads are better than one, and four eyes are better than two.

If you are transitioning or are recently discharged from the military, you will need to do a little strategic planning as it relates to your resume. Here's a simple word of advice: Focus on your technical and managerial competencies that are relevant to the type of civilian position you are seeking, and you will have an idea of what type of resume format to choose.

Before you decide which format you want to use, let's examine the most popular resume formats: chronological, functional, combination, targeted, and curriculum vitae. Each has pros and cons.

1. Chronological Resume Format

A chronological resume format starts by chronologically listing your work history, with the most recent position listed first.

Your academic education is listed at the end. This is particularly effective if you have consistently moved to increasingly better jobs, with no significant periods of unemployment. Employers typically prefer this type of resume because it's easy to see what jobs you have held and when you have held them. However, it does not always make it easier to fulfill your objective—getting the interview. Although this resume format is preferred by most selecting departments, it would be beneficial to you to evaluate its pros and cons and conclude if it would be effective for you.

Pros:
- It is easy to read and easy to highlight positions you have held.
- Shows your job stability if you have not changed jobs
- It describes your roles and achievements.
- It reflects an increase in your responsibilities and/or promotions.
- Easier to seek work like your current position
- It highlights employment with impressive or important companies.

Cons:
- It calls attention to your change of company.
- It may reveal your age.
- It may show a lack of recycling or updated training.
- It reflects periods of inactivity or activity that is irrelevant for the position.

2. Functional Resume Format

A functional resume format highlights your skills and accomplishments rather than focusing on your chronological work history. You extract your achievements and skills from the experience section and position them together at the top of the resume in a section titled "Accomplishments" or "Capabilities." This focuses the potential employer's attention on what you can do or have done rather than where or when you have worked. Only after impressing the employer with your accomplishments and skills do you present your work history as part of a brief format with dates. This format is used most often by individuals who are changing careers, have changed jobs often, or who have significant gaps in their employment history.

Pros:
- It features your abilities and knowledge that are most relevant to the position you want to attain.
- Because it doesn't tell your life story chronologically, it disguises periods of inactivity or successive similar jobs without promotion.
- It focuses on the fact that you can do the work even if you have no job experience actually doing it, an important point if you gained the skills serving in the military or while doing volunteer work.
- It eliminates the role repetition in similar positions.
- It helps to disguise your age, which cannot legally be a barrier to employment but often is as a practical matter. It

also helps hide the fact that you have recently graduated from college or a trade school.
- It is useful in new technologies, internet, telecommunications, media, and publicity fields.

Cons:
- It does not emphasize the names of the companies for which you have worked.
- It does not stress the length of time each position was held. (This could be important with employers seeking a long-term employee.)
- It limits the description of the positions you have held and their responsibilities.

> "Seest thou a man diligent in his business? He shall stand before kings; he shall not stand before mean men."
> ~ Proverbs 22:29 KJV

3. Combination Resume Format

A combination resume format includes elements of the chronological and functional formats. It summarizes your skills and accomplishments first, with your employment history listed next. The combination format is more difficult to write and more complex, but it highlights your skills related to the job you are applying for and provides the work history that employers prefer.

Pros:
- It shows very clearly that you know what you want to do and that you have the skills necessary to get the job done.
- It gives you more flexibility and creativity in describing your abilities.
- It helps to obtain a particular position.
- It eliminates information about your abilities and experience that you may prefer to exclude if you are applying for more than one position in the same company.

Cons:
- You need a different summary for each job that you choose.
- It is time-consuming.

4. Targeted Resume Format

A targeted resume format is customized so that it specifically highlights the experience and skills you have that are relevant to the job you are applying for. It is like the combination format in that it lists skills first followed by job experience. However, while the combination format can be used for many job openings with minor changes, the targeted format is very specific to the one job you are seeking. It is more complex and labor-intensive because you must ensure that you have included as many details as possible about how your key skills relate to the job you are applying for, but it is a popular one to use.

Keep these tips in mind when using the targeted resume format:

- Position the summary of qualifications or career highlights section at the top of your resume.
- Mirror your experience, credentials, and education to the job description; include it in the summary of qualifications section at the top of your resume.
- Last, list your experience in reverse chronological order, just like you would on a traditional resume.

Pros:

- It works well for you when you have extensive experience in your job target.
- The format provides visual breaks and is attractive to the reader.

Cons:

- It may be difficult to convey strengths in a career transition.

Sample Functional Resume

Frank House
PO Box 21
Tyler, TX 55552
Telephone (555) 555-5513
Email: frank.henderson@disney.net

Objective: To attain marketing position that will utilize my writing skills and enable me to make a positive contribution.

Note: Use related key words for positions you are applying for in the objective section and in the rest of the resume.

Skills and Abilities

Writing
- Produced a variety of business materials, including letters, reports, proposals, and forms
- Formulated employee policy manuals and job descriptions
- Proofread and edited all referenced written materials

Marketing
- Designed, developed, and implemented marketing and sales campaigns, fundraisers, employee incentive programs and contests
- Evaluated target markets and proposed marketing strategies

- Managed all phases of direct mail projects; monitored production teams; recruited and guided vendors; oversaw print operations and coordinated mailing process

Communication
- Established and improved client communications; maintained ongoing relationships
- Addressed customer inquiries; interpreted and delivered information; proposed suggestions; provided guidance; identified, investigated, and negotiated conflicts
- Conducted surveys and analyzed results

Business Administrative and Management
- Hired, trained, coached, supervised, and evaluated staff members
- Launched and operated sole proprietorship
- Achieved computer proficiency; demonstrated knowledge of Microsoft Word, Excel, PowerPoint, Publisher, Adobe Photoshop, and all internet functions

Education and Training
- Park College (University Online)
- BA in English-Professional Writing
- Certificate Technical Writing
- Anticipated Graduation in mid-2008
- Current GPA: 4.0 (on scale of 4.0)

Employment
- 01/2003—present, Freelance Writer/Administrative

- 04/1999—07/2000, Enrollment Specialist, Sales Coordinator, Tyler, Texas
- 08/2000—03/2003, Project Manager, Print & Mail Advertising, Tyler, Texas
- 04/2003—12/2006, CEO & Owner, Capital Marketing Inc., Tyler, Texas

References Available Upon Request

Functional Resume Format
Landed Jane Doe Her Ideal Job

Jane, a skilled sales professional, was unsure which resume format to use. She discussed it with me at length and decided that the functional resume format would better fit the job she wanted. Jane said that the functional format better emphasized her skills and capabilities and gave her choices as to the career areas where she wanted to work. The result? She got the job.

5. Curriculum Vitae (CV) Format

A curriculum vitae (CV) is different than a resume. The word "vitae" is Latin for "life," and the curriculum vitae consists of a compilation of all the academic data and experience of a person throughout his or her life. Generally, the CV is used in Europe, Asia, and Africa. The CV is accepted in American academic, science, medical, research, and technology positions. Normally it is not specific to the position for which you are applying. Its structure includes personal data, academic achievements, experience, languages, computer science, and other data, all placed in chronological order. Its layout consists of the following sections: objective, education, experience, additional information, and reference. Naturally, it is much longer than a resume.

How to Turn Your CV into an Effective Resume
There are important points to consider when converting your CV into an effective resume. First, you must make certain that your CV is clear, concise, complete, and up-to-date with current employment and educational information. Remember, your objective is to get the interview, so you can convince the interviewer that you are the perfect candidate for the position. Second, you must show that you have the specific experience, achievements, and skills for the position you want. Also, you should omit the academic and/or work experience that is not related to the job you want, or at least summarize it in a phrase. When you successfully write your CV this way, it shows that you satisfy the characteristics required to perform the job for which you are applying.

Curriculum Vitae (CV)

Joan Van Arc
(111) 222-0000
anywhereusa.com

Education

September 2007, University of Texas, Denton, Texas
- Bachelor of Science in Environmental Engineering degree (EE)
- Major academic courses highlights: Company Property Management, Marketing, Economics, English
- Technology Communication, Information Management System, Modern Fabrication System

May 2006—Certified Public Accounting (CPA) Training

Occupation

December 2006—present, ITT TECH investment, Dallas, Texas
Application Engineer, Sales & Marketing
- Application support and industry projects tracing to sales office to achieve the sales budget and new industry market application research
- Pay suitable visits to end users and DI for seminars and technical presentations with salesperson or distributors while collecting marketing information and competitor information analysis

July 2005—November 2006, Intel Products Co., Dallas, Texas
CPU Assembly Engineer
- Analyzed the yield-ratio trend, documented and solved the current problems
- Participated in the training of marketing, business process modeling, and analysis at Intel University
- Visualized a project review with impressive presentation and multimedia animation, which was highly appreciated by department manager

June 2003—June 2005, GE Bank Corp., LTD
Student Intern
- Analyzed investment principles of related financial derived products
- Formulated the scheme of market popularization and network marketing

Awards, Competencies, & Interests
English Ability: Band 6 and the intermediate test of interpretation

Computer Skills:
National Computer Level 3 Certificate (Network Communication)
C++, JMP, AutoCAD, 3ds Max, Photoshop

Personal Interests:
Basketball (skills); skating (speed); English (elegant); snooker (stable)

Secrets to Developing a Power-Packed Resume
You are almost ready to turn your skills and assets into a killer resume. Before you do, I want to let you in on the three most important secrets that professional resume writers know are the keys to writing an effective resume.

RESUME Trade Secret #1:
A Concise, Precise Job Objective
The job objective quickly tells the employer (or the person reviewing the resume) whether your resume is worth reading. It must be direct and to the point because employers don't have time to read every resume from beginning to end. If you have a weak objective, or no objective your resume possibly won't be read. Writing a short, precise objective makes the employer's task easier because it allows him or her to focus only on resumes from people who really want the job and whose qualifications are most relevant to the position. Remember, you must catch the eye of an employer in a few seconds.

When writing a concise job objective, consider the following tips:

- **Focus on employers' needs**—Word your objective so that you seem exactly like the perfect fit. Research the company and the job announcement to craft a compelling objective that perfectly aligns with the employer's needs.
- **Avoid being vague and using clichés**—Tailor your objective to the specific job you are applying for. Instead of saying, "obtaining an entry-level position," use the specific job title on the announcement. Also, instead of using general terms

like "communication skills," use specific descriptions such as "technical writing" or "telemarketing skills." This shows that you are precise and that you know what you want.

RESUME Trade Secret #2:
Using Effective Branding Strategies

Your first impression is a lasting one, so your resume and cover letter must grab the employer's attention. As with newspaper ads and magazines, **headlines are a winner.** This is an optional strategy. When used effectively, it can charm prospective employers and inspire them to read your entire resume.

***Sample Headlines*:**
- "Skilled Negotiator Secures Another Multimillion-dollar Contract... with Ease." (You can use this headline to boast about your past sales experience).
- "Profit-Driven Executive—Strong Customer Focus"

RESUME Trade Secret #3:
Playing the Numbers Game

The information in the previous sections outlined ways to speak an employer's language: numbers as they relate to profits.

There is another numbers game—the age game, and it's a game you might have to find creative ways to win if you are older or younger than the typical person who the employer expects to hire for a position. While government regulations may prohibit age discrimination, we all know it happens, and it's not hard to hide if it occurs when an employer is sifting through a stack of resumes. The goal is to get past that stage to the interview, where you can sell an employer on your qualifications and where age discrimination would be more obvious and overt.

How do you win the age game? You can do this by making your age less obvious on your resume. To illustrate, let's say that you are seeking an executive or managerial position that normally goes to people in their midtwenties to midthirties, but you are in your late forties. You can delete ten years of your earliest experience to give the appearance that you are younger. Think of it this way: Employers figure most people graduate college or enter the workforce around the age of 22. Therefore, if they see 25-plus years of experience on your resume, they assume you are around the age of 47. But if they see only 10 to 12 years of experience on your resume, then they will assume that you are around the age of 32 or 34.

It works the other way too. Suppose you have recently graduated from college, and you do not want to appear too young on your resume. In this case, you will need to gather information from your high school and college days, thus bringing your perceived age up 5 or 10 years. The employer will think you are at least 27 or 32 years old. Stay open for ways to strategically make yourself marketable as opportunity awaits you.

STEP IV—GETTING NOTICED

Posting Your Resume

"Seest thou a man diligent in his business? He shall stand before kings; he shall not stand before mean men."
—Proverbs 22:29 KJV

In a competitive market, you must develop effective strategies to gain an advantage over your competitors—other job seekers. However, winning strategies alone won't help if you don't know where to look for the lucrative jobs.

Some job seekers are intimidated about applying for six-figure jobs because they seem rare. They believe that only doctors, lawyers, and CEOs make that kind of money when, in fact, many six-figure jobs require skills and experience, not a graduate degree. Knowing where to find those jobs puts you ahead of the game, so turn yourself into an investigative reporter and prepare to write your own life story. With diligence and persistence, your work will pay off.

Where to Begin?

Start by researching your prospective employers. For each company, ask yourself the following questions:

- What does this corporation do?
- How long has this corporation been in existence?
- Who are its competitors?
- Who are the senior staff and officers within this company?
- What are the products and/or services?
- Are there corporate/industry problems and predictions of mergers, acquisitions, pending lawsuits, and bankruptcies?
- How big is this corporation?
- How does this corporation stand out among its competitors?

Remember, it's better to discover an unpleasant answer to one of these questions before you accept a job with a company and not after.

Reference Resources

Where should you begin your research? The first step is to determine if a company is publicly held (traded on a stock exchange), privately owned (not listed on a stock exchange), or a subsidiary of a publicly held corporation. This will simplify the research process. The law requires publicly held companies to report certain financial information to the Securities and Exchange Commission (SEC) and their shareholders (those who have a stake in the company). Contacting corporate officers or top management members through online and published directories is helpful.

Another recommendation is to contact the marketing or public relations department and request an annual report. Most public organizations produce in-house newsletters, so request copies of these as well as other published materials through their public affairs office.

Check to see if the Office of Public Liaison at any federal government agency can send you information about a public organization where you wish to work. Make sure it contains the agency's mission, history, budget, programs, and type of work. County and city governments publish handbooks and publications including extensive demographic information. Check with your local government agencies or visit your library or online library resource to find them. These can be useful resources.

Published Resources—Library

Although some view them as old school, libraries contain a wealth of information to help you with your job search. Each library is different, and some will be more helpful to you than others. Regional, larger public, and college libraries tend to have a large variety of business and general periodical indexes, business and technical journals, and newspapers. Many libraries have access to the internet and directories (database systems) with extensive information about major corporations (more about this later). Some may perform searches for you for free or for a small fee it is well worth the cost. Check the nearest professional and trade associations and inquire if they have specialized libraries that you can use.

If you do not have access to a large public library or a college or university library, then your hometown library still is a great resource. At the very least, it can be an effective supplement to a tool that gets better every day–digital libraries.

Digital Libraries

Digital libraries, or virtual libraries, are the internet's version of the public library. Here are a few of the most useful.

- Open Library (https://openlibrary.org)—Go to the "Reference" section and look under the "Business Directories" category. The "Business Directories" or "Employment" subcategories have links to company-related information.
- Archive.Org (https://archive.org)—Go to the "Business Directories" section and look under Topics and Subjects category (connect to the "Careers-General, Job Hunting, Directories, Corporations United States Directories, etc.) in "Business" section of the site.

There are millions of websites on the internet that contain a vast amount of job information. Unfortunately, unlike the library, the information is not neatly arranged, so you will need to rely heavily on popular search tools such as Yahoo (yahoo.com), Google (google.com), and Ask (ask.com) or if you have a particular search tool that works for you. Links to some popular websites for finding six-figure jobs are www.indeed.com, www.clearedconnections.com, and www.salary.com.

Whether you are looking for a job or preparing for a job interview, consider letting the internet be your guide in finding the right career for you. You can find recruiters and companies in your profession or desired profession as well as your desired geographical area. Once you find a contact for the job you want, you can start to build your networking prospects (review Step II, Networking) and create new networking channels with those recruiters and with prospective employers.

Corporate Directories

Corporate directories contain valuable information about thousands of companies and are available online and in hard-copy form. *Hoover's Handbook of American Business 2018* (can be located under catalogs or directories or you can order on www.amazon.com); *The Directory of Corporate Affiliations* (www.corporateaffiliations.com); *Dunn and Bradstreet's Million Dollar Databases*; and the *Thomas Register* are some of the most useful. Always verify the information, because companies, and the names of your most important contacts, often change between updates.

Hoover's is a good resource that covers the world's biggest, fastest-growing, and most influential enterprises with four publications: *Hoover's Handbook of American Business*; *Hoover's Handbook of Emerging Companies*; *Hoover's Handbook of World*

Business; and *Hoover's Handbook of Private Companies* provide information about millions of companies and industries, as well as the people who lead them. This database also contains a current listing of Fortune 500 companies. You'll need to pay a subscription fee to use this website from your personal computer, but your local library may have free access, or you can research these resources in eBook format through openlibrary.org.

NRP Direct (nrpdirect.com/NRP) publishes the *Directory of Corporate Affiliations* and is a leading provider of business reference information. It provides an in-depth view of more than 15,000 public and private businesses and their divisions, subsidiaries, and domestic and worldwide affiliates with revenues in excess of $8 million or workforces in excess of 250. It also lists non-U.S. based companies with revenues in excess of $45 million. The information includes mergers, acquisitions, and name changes, and is updated annually. So, this is just a basic source of information you can start with and build on for your career and business goals.

Likewise, *Dunn and Bradstreet's Million Dollar Databases* includes information on 150,000 U.S. businesses that process at least $8 million in sales volume. The information is updated annually.

Thomas Publishing Company (thomasnet.com) produces the *Thomas Register*, which contains profiles of more than 100,000 U.S. companies including corporate addresses, telephone numbers, asset ratings, company executives, sales office locations, plants, and subsidiaries/division and product line information. The information is updated annually.

Direct Research Method

Companies prefer that you approach them directly, so it's a good idea to contact corporate officers or top management members via their website and published directories. I call this the Direct Research Method. This strategy involves going directly to a company's website and applying online or by email for jobs. This is another effective way of establishing rapport before you send your resume. One thing you should keep in mind: Although you have some level of control here, you must have a clear vision as to what you want and what career interests you are pursuing because employers are not interested in playing "career matchmaker."

How to Use the Direct Research Method

Once you have found the organization(s) that interest you, investigate a little further to identify the appropriate hiring manager. This can be revealed through the company's website, other sources on the internet, directories, networking, or by calling the company directly. Make sure you get the correct spelling of that person's name and his or her exact job title.

Next, write a letter with a catchy headline and a charming layout or a layout that is easy on the eyes. This means you should try and go with a layout that gives a balance of white space and helps as the person reviewing your resume sees it in a professional way. Remember anything you send reflects you. Use a short paragraph to summarize your experience and achievements, quickly demonstrating that you have a lot to offer. Make sure that you have information about your recent position and sum up your letter; state you are interested in meeting with the person. This gives you a certain level of control: You can continue with the communication by following up, or you can let the communication die. You choose. If you are unsure as to how to use the Direct Research Method in your letter to the hiring manager(s), corporate officers, or top management members, refer to the samples in this section.

Here's an example:

Jon Doe
555 Sunny Brook Lane
Wizard Oaks, KS 55516
(555) 121–0000
Email: joe@yellowbrickroad.com

WIZARD INDUSTRIES, INC.
Tin Mann Anderson
HR, Escort Dorothy
333 Toto Ave.
Bismarck, KS 55526

January 4, 2019

Dear Mr. Anderson:

Do you want to increase your company's profit margin sales in the next six months? Your competition does. As organizations strive to improve profitability and productivity while maintaining a competitive edge, there is a growing need for senior executives who can manage change and transition while strengthening their bottom lines. I am a results-oriented leader who successfully directed telecommunications companies through a dynamic and turbulent business environment.

My accomplishments include:
- Doubled annual sales revenue
- Developed and implemented leading-edge services
- Devised successful marketing programs to target, penetrate, and acquire new business

I am seeking a new challenge and am interested in relocating to the Bismarck area. I will be in Bismarck on February 1, 2019. I will call to set up an appointment.

Sincerely,
Jon Doe

Dos and Don'ts in Using the Direct Research Method

Dos:
- Use positive statements such as, "My background and experience make me a perfect fit for this job"—and then show how.
- Provide your phone number and inform the recipient that you will follow up with a call.

Don'ts:
- Don't write statements in your letter requesting the receiver to refer you to someone in the event there is no opening; in most cases (not all), the receiver won't recommend someone they do not know.

> "I can do all things through Christ, which strengthens me."
> ~ Philippians 4:13 KJV

- Never use negative statements like, "I realize that I may not have the exact experience for the job." These kinds of statements downplay your letter.
- Don't use statements that appear you are asking the receiver to research job openings for you. For example, "I am requesting any possible assistance you can give concerning my pursuit of a job opening with your company."

Jack Gets the Job He Wants Using the Direct Research Method

Jack had recently retired from the military but wanted to continue working in a job that allowed him to practice the skills he had learned in the service. He had tried to post his resume on various websites without success, so he approached me with a list of jobs he wanted to target. He wanted to know how to get noticed. During several counseling sessions, I learned the kind of job he sought, the location, and the company size.

I coached Jack on using the Direct Research Method. Two weeks later, he was singing a new song. He landed the position he wanted with one of the companies, KBR-Halliburton, that we had targeted.

STEP V— PUT YOUR BEST FOOT FORWARD

The Interview

"I can do all things through Christ, which strengthens me"
—Philippians 4:13 KJV

As we discussed earlier, the hiring process at most companies involves extensive planning. In fact, it can be months between the time an employee announces he is leaving and the time that position is open to you. Meanwhile, employers look for current employees to fill that job. So, when you go to your next job interview, remember that the position for which you are interviewing was typically planned and budgeted for well in advance.

The Employment Interview—What is It?

The basic purpose or objective of an employment interview is the attainment of desired information through effective communication. Employers set up interviews to determine if a candidate has specific qualities they are looking for to fill positions within their companies.

There is nothing new or unusual about the interview process. You do it all the time in your professional and personal life (dating can be a similar example. If you have children, you would want to consider interviewing the daycare provider or company to ensure they are the right fit for handling your little angels' needs).

Mastering the employment interview during a job search is simply a matter of being aware of the process and tapping into your inner strength to overcome any hindrances that you may have. The more you understand, the more confident you will be. There's a saying to the effect that a person fears what they do not understand and embraces what they can relate to.

Mastering interviewing takes great patience and much attention to the process and the people involved. Unfortunately, there is no shortcut to learning, nor does one successful interview make a person proficient.

Interview Preparation

Mental conditioning is an important aspect in preparing for an interview. You must feel confident in order to convey positive impressions to the interviewer. If you do not feel confident or if you are nervous and afraid, the interviewer will know.

Some interviewees might equate interviewing to confronting Goliath, but remember this: Just as David prevailed, so shall you. So, take the necessary steps to prepare so you will not be caught off guard, and remember to never let the Goliaths see you sweat.

A helpful suggestion in interview preparation is consider hiring or reaching out to an interview coach who can help you practice and be prepared before your big day—the interview. He or she can be a resource to helping you get comfortable and more confident about the interview process. He or she may offer helpful tips for the interview and future ones as you move up the career ladder. Consider investing in yourself. You are worth it!

"Fire" Your Fear

It's not uncommon for job seekers to fear interviewing, but you don't have to live with fear any more than an employer must live with a lazy employee. How can you "fire" your fear? Some psychologists believe that facing fears is the first step in driving them away. Cognitive behavioral therapy (CBT), which focuses on changing a person's thoughts or mindset in order to change behavior, can help some people overcome depression and low self-esteem. Try CBT exercises; see if it works for you. The added advantage is that it would reduce fear, and you won't have to take pills to do an interview!

I hold fast to a passage in the Bible that encourages me to take my thoughts captive and reign over negative thoughts that try to hold me back (2 Corinthians 10:5, KJV). Bad thoughts lead to bad feelings and serves no one. Specifically, Proverbs 23:7, KJV in the Bible states, "As a man thinketh in his heart, so is he." So, see yourself as a conqueror. I encourage you to find that process that works for you.

Firing Your Fear Exercise for Job Seekers:

1. Know what you are fearful of and why.

2. Then ask basic questions, such as:
   - What will happen if I don't get the job?
   - What's the worst that can happen?
   - How will it feel to look back and laugh when I get this job?
   - How great will life look if I get this job?

3. Prioritize your fears from the smallest to the greatest. This will help you sort through unnecessary fears. Write down ten different circumstances and categorize them from moderate to intense.

4. Now, put yourself in each of those situations, starting with the easiest ones first. Face each item in sequence. Consider a simple breathing exercise tip like focusing on quieting your inner thoughts and take slow, deep breaths. As you take slow, deep breaths inhaling the air around you, allow your abdominal muscles to push outward. Remember inhale air and exhale or push stomach muscles outward to give you a

balance and help your Lungs. I find this breathing tip helpful when I need to clear my thoughts and to calm myself.

5. Record your response in a journal to help you confront a recurring fear. Later, you can evaluate and see what you did to overcome it.

Try these exercises 10 to 15 minutes a day, and you should see noticeable results within a matter of a few short weeks because you have formed a habit that helps you eliminate your fears. However, keep in mind that these are suggestions—not prescribed formulas set in stone. If you feel you need additional help in this area to confront and handle anxiety, seek out professional counseling. You can visit the Anxiety Disorders of America website at adaa.org.

Other Ways to Prepare for Your Next Interview

Meditation

Meditation helps calm the mind and increases your confidence. What you pay the most attention to is what will affect your mental makeup, so meditation can be a valuable self-help tool to prepare for your next interview. When you find yourself stressed, meditate or stay quiet for 5 to 10 minutes so you can draw strength from resting or calming your inner thoughts.

One approach I like to use for my meditation is the quietness method. This form of meditation can help ease your mind and dispel uneasiness. Trying this method, you would simply quiet your inner thoughts and begin to think about peaceful things like a flowing stream or a sweet-smelling flower. Continue this process until you notice results in your thoughts and behavior. Try this approach consistently and notice how it can make a difference.

Visualization
Visualizing is using your imagination to picture what you want before you get it. Imagine yourself in an intense final interview with the officers of one of the most successful companies in the world, and at the end, they enthusiastically shake your hand and offer you the job. Write down how you felt while rehearsing the interview. Tackle any negative emotions so you'll know how to confront them if they surface. Remember take your negative thoughts captive and be the conqueror in your mind, will, and emotions (2 Corinthians 10:5, KJV).

You can create other visualization exercises for yourself. I've found that prayer and the previously mentioned exercise to be uplifting. Choose what works for you. If when visualizing your success, you can't see mental pictures, don't worry. Sometimes acceptance from your intuitive state may come in the form of a strong feeling or a deep thought. Either way, you are planting the visualizing concept in your mind. As you practice this method, you'll find that visualization will become increasingly easier.

Physical Appearance and Mannerisms
Interviews can happen at any time. A chance conversation at a bank, a grocery store, or a restaurant can open the door

to the job or career of your dreams. So, it is up to you to invest in yourself.

Dress each day as if you are going for an interview. This will help create consistency in your life and keep you physically and mentally confident. Always keep at least two perfectly clean suits or garments prepared because you never know if an accident may happen with one of them. Women who are challenged financially can add a scarf or a pendant to their garment to jazz it up, while men can wear a nice tie or a collared shirt. This inexpensive gesture can make you feel better about yourself and make a lasting difference. But don't focus so much on your appearance that you detract from your communication. Your appearance and mannerisms should focus attention on what you say and do, not on what you wear.

A first impression is a lasting impression. Remember that how you look has an important bearing on how another person will respond to you. For instance, if you project that you are confident and competent, it will greatly increase your success in an interview. Establishing trust is a critical step in this process. Focus on being as natural as possible. Because what is natural to one person may not be to another; develop your own style and be consistent with it. People are generally quick to sense artificiality and will view you with suspicion. Practice nonverbal gestures until you feel you are communicating naturally, and your movements flow smoothly. Remember to maintain good eye contact. Looking away, particularly at critical moments, can lead a listener to believe that you don't value or believe what you have conveyed.

Transportation

If you do not secure reliable transportation for your interview, you risk the chance of missing that rewarding career opportunity. Employers terminate employees for not showing up to work, so they certainly won't hire you if you miss an interview no matter your excuse. Being late for an interview can determine your destiny and will likely mean that you won't land your dream job. Being late for an interview is like being late for a bus. It will move on without you.

Most important, know your tardiness, in other words, can hold up others. So be on time—better yet—be early. You never know how it will turn out unless you make the interview. So, don't chance it. If you do not drive, make sure that you have arranged reliable transportation for getting back and forth to your soon-to-be job. Explore creative options and have a contingency plan if this is a problem.

Transportation Contingency Plan
- Public transportation (ensure it is close to work area)
- Carpooling
- Motorcycle (if you ride one)
- Bicycle (during moderate weather)
- Uber or Lyft (only when you really need it)
- Close friend's vehicle (make sure you pay for gas)

Using the SWOT Analysis

Preparing for the interview is a very important process. It empowers you and gives you the opportunity to be proactive.

But first, you should take time to assess yourself. One technique is a Self-SWOT Analysis, or SSWOTA. SWOT is short for strengths, weaknesses, opportunities, and threats. Businesses use the SWOT analysis to evaluate their worth and strategically plan, and you should, too, if you plan to move ahead.

Before taking the SWOT challenge, it would help you to understand its purpose. From a business perspective, the SWOT analysis is a scan of internal and external environments. Strengths and weaknesses are internal elements, while opportunities and threats are external elements. A SWOT analysis helps companies match their resources and capabilities to that of their competitors and carve a sustainable niche in their market(s). A SSWOTA can help you uncover opportunities that you never realized existed while allowing you to eliminate and manage threats that otherwise could catch you off guard.

Preparing Your Self-SWOT Analysis

Many clients say the thought of preparing a SSWOTA makes them feel uneasy. But the truth is: they are presented with a verbal SSWOTA whenever they interview. It may appear in various forms, but it is a SSWOTA just the same. Therefore, it is best to be prepared.

Remember, the basic questions involved in a SSWOTA are:
- What are my strengths?
- What are my weaknesses?
- What are my opportunities?
- What are my threats?

You need to focus on your strengths and weaknesses because those are internal elements over which you have more control. Opportunities and threats are external elements over which you have less control. Responses should be incorporated into your SSWOTA model (see example below).

Become more familiar with the SSWOTA, and you will find that your responses in live interviews will flow smoothly and with ease. You will be able to knowledgeably describe your strengths to your prospective employer, which will give that person insight as to your suitability for the company. You also will be able to ask questions about the company that pertain to you, giving you more control over the interview process and helping decipher possible opportunities and threats. Practice pays off. Remember: the interviewer wants to see the real you.

Elements Incorporated in a SSWOTA

What are my strengths?
- Core competencies (i.e., expertise, abilities, proficiencies)
- Experience and education
- Personal competitive advantage among peers
- Financial status
- Reputation, philosophy, and values
- Strong networking (professional/personal) to make contacts and garner support.

What are my weaknesses? (Do you feel inexperienced, unqualified, untrained, and unskilled?)

- Lack competitive strength
- Reputation, presence, image
- Vulnerabilities: cultural, attitudinal, and behavioral
- Location, geographical (mobility)
- Gaps in mission-critical skills

What are my opportunities?
- Support system(s): family, peers, and other
- Strategic development, information, research, and findings
- Technology development and innovation
- Peers/superior vulnerabilities

What are my threats?
- Aggressive competition (other job seekers, others competing for the same contracts)
- Personal limitations
- Corporate culture politics
- Unpredictable changes to career/business

Rules for a Successful SSWOTA:
- Be truthful about your strengths and weaknesses. It's your SSWOTA.
- Make sure your SSWOTA is short and to the point. Keep it simple.

Self-SWOT Analysis Table

Use this table to conduct your SWOT analysis. Every area of the SWOT should be examined to achieve maximum benefit.

	Your Weaknesses	Threats	
	Your Strengths	Opportunities	
	Internal/Personal	External/SWOT	

The Interview in Action Role-Playing Exercise
With interviewing, as with most things in life, practice makes perfect. When you practice answering questions a potential employer is likely to ask, you will fluently speak the language of interviewing—even while feeling nervous. Having rehearsed your answers will help you field questions naturally and with confidence.

Planning and preparing are key tips for ensuring you lay effective groundwork for the interview process. It pays to be prepared. Planning what to wear and what to bring with you to the interview is a good way of planning ahead and ensuring that you don't spend unnecessary time rushing on the day of your interview. Another effective way to prepare is to rehearse. Mock interviews are a good way to prepare. Mock interviews with a friend or a family member are one of the best ways to prepare for the big day. Conducting mock interviews will help you prepare effective responses; it can be an important tool in revealing areas in which you need more practice. For example, if you need to rehearse pitching your accomplishments, you can craft your responses while conducting mock interviews and receive feedback to revise and improve upon your answers. Or if you tend to speak quickly—especially when nervous—you can practice slowing down your speech and speaking confidently at a measured pace.

Another useful exercise that prepares you for interviewing is perception checking. Here's how it works: You begin by speaking for about three minutes, which is approximated at 5 to 10 sentences. You can choose any topic—it doesn't have to be job-related. When you are finished, your conversation partner repeats back to you what he or she thought they heard you say, using statements such as, "Let me make sure I understood you correctly. It sounded as if you said . . ." The original speaker clarifies anything that was misinterpreted. Reverse roles so that both people have an opportunity to speak and listen. Again, if you misunderstand what the speaker is trying to say, you both work to clarify the message.

I have found this exercise to be very beneficial. It helps improve your active listening skills, which involves listening to a speaker and then summarizing their key points. With consistent practice, you learn to show respect to the speaker while demonstrating that you understand what he or she is saying. It also improves your speaking skills by teaching you when you are most often misinterpreted so that you can devise more effective communication methods.

Types of Interviews

The Informational Interview

Informational interviews are interviews in which you, the job seeker, initiate the meeting to exchange information and make acquaintance with a potential employer without reference to a specific job opening. It gives you the opportunity to explore career fields and learn about jobs you might pursue. This type of interview can be your key to success. Unfortunately, job seekers use informational interviewing far too infrequently. Treat this type of interview as if you are interviewing for a

job coordinated by the hiring manager and come prepared with thoughtful questions about the field and the company.
Samples questions for you to ask include:
- What experience, skills, and education are required for the job?
- What do you like or dislike about your job?
- What are the current problems or challenges facing this industry today?

Initiating this type of interview gives you a distinct advantage. You can confirm with the prospective employer if you have the required qualifications for the job you are seeking, and if not, you can ask for advice on how to position yourself for future job openings (if there are none available at the moment). Before you leave the informational interview, obtain references. Ask the interviewer if he or she would be comfortable if you contact other people and use his or her name. Give that person your card, contact information, and resume. Afterward, send a thank-you letter by email.

Employers who like to stay acquainted with available talent, even when they have no job openings, are most often receptive to informational interviews. Informational interviews also work well if the employer likes sharing their knowledge or values the mutual friend who made the introduction.

One-on-One Interview

The one-on-one interview–one interviewer with one job candidate—is the most common type. The interviewer takes one of two approaches during this type of interview: direct or indirect. The indirect style is less structured with the interviewer having some level of flexibility in the questions they ask. The direct style involves a clear agenda and a uniform set of questions asked of all candidates to compare results more easily. The interviewer asks specific questions about work experience, career goals, education, training, skills, or community, personal, and leisure activities. Potential questions include, "What career goals have you set for yourself?" and "What experience have you had with the computer industry?" Remember to recognize the pattern the interviewer sets and follow his or her lead. Do not get frustrated and give up if you feel tense during the interview. You still have some control over the interviewing process. Remember that you're interviewing the company as much as the company is interviewing you! You're trying to determine if the company is a good fit for you.

Sam Peak, a client of mine, came to me for career guidance and help in preparing for his interview. Sam told me that his dream was eventually to own a landscaping business with 40 employees. I could see that his career plan was detailed, but the nagging issue—which was one of the reasons he came to see me—was that he had a limited amount of experience.

Sam did not have any apprehensions about working for someone else. In fact, he stated that he wanted to gain experience from his soon-to-be competitor so that he later could branch out on his own. Sam's dilemma was how would he prepare for his upcoming face-to-face interview with the owner of the company?

Sam and I trained diligently, and he came out smelling like a rose. He learned a lot of lessons during his training, but he attributed his landing the job to his 30-second commercial response, a technique for responding to tough questions.

The 30-second elevator pitch—the equivalent of a soundbite in radio and television—is a statement, 30 seconds or less, that describes your skills and professional experience that apply to the job for which you are interviewing. (You can also create them for other areas of your life.) Craft your 30-second commercial response and then practice, practice, practice to keep it precise and appealing. Thirty seconds may seem like a short amount of time, but it is long enough not only to attract your prospective employer's attention but also to persuade him or her to hire you. If you speak any longer, you risk being tuned out. A powerful 30-second commercial response can put you in the driver's seat and change the course of your career and your life.

Back to the story about Sam. When I asked Sam what question and response had helped him land him the job, he said that it was when the owner asked him, "Why should I hire you to work for me?"

"I can do the job; I don't let the grass grow under my feet," he had replied. "I can eliminate your need for an extra employee. You would benefit from having a valuable employee who has experience in landscaping. I perform many duties, such as trimming and pruning hedges, trees, and shrubs; planting, transplanting, and maintaining flowers, plants, greenhouse and nursery stock; seeding, sodding, and caring for lawns; consulting with clients on landscape designs; and plant selection and care and more. You would gain more service requests from clients, which increases your revenue and market presence. I have a proven track record for profitable results. This can be an asset to your company. I'd like to produce similar results for ABC Landscaping. I can cover ground fast, so don't delay in contacting me. I look forward to a positive response."

I train my clients to respond intellectually to their interviewer. I teach them to build rapport and to grab the interviewer's attention by offering appealing responses like Sam's that entice the interviewer. With practice, you can give a job-winning answer like Sam's.

The Panel Interview

The panel interview is another common interview. This is used most frequently in the public sector as well as in companies that rely heavily on teamwork. In this type of setting, two or more interviewers question candidates in hopes of filling a job opening within their organization. Normally, the panel includes a representative from human resources, the hiring manager, and someone associated with the department that is filling the position. The questions are typically preselected so that every candidate is asked the same questions. When the interviewing process is completed, panelists rank the candidates, and the one with the highest ranking is offered the job.

Many job candidates find this interview style intimidating. Instead of focusing their attention on one interviewer, they must face a room full of interrogators. It can be nerve-racking, especially if there is no advance warning of a panel interview.

But if you know how to respond, you can ace this interview and be offered the job of your dreams.

Helpful Tips for Mastering the Panel Interview
- Be prepared psychologically to expend more energy and be more alert than you would be in a one-on-one interview.
- Relax and appear calm and confident.
- Recognize the important figures or members on the panel and distinguish which role each one is fulfilling. (Try doing this when introductions are made, remembering that the chairperson is usually the one who makes the introductions.)
- Identify the person to whom you would be reporting directly.
- Treat each person as an important individual.
- When asked a question, make eye contact with each person and speak directly to the one who asked the question.
- Ask for each person's business card before you leave the interview.
- Stay focused and adaptable.

Behavioral-Based Interview
In behavioral-based interviews, potential employers ask specific questions about how you have performed or behaved in past situations in order to assess if you have the skills they are seeking. You will be asked to describe specific situations in which you were required to use your problem-solving, leadership, conflict resolution, or multitasking skills. Your responses will require thought and organization. Be prepared

to answer open-ended and closed-ended questions. An open-ended question often begins with words such as "describe," or "when." An example is: "Describe a time you responded to an irate customer." Closed-ended questions seek yes or no answers and are used mostly to verify or confirm information about the job seeker. An example is, "You have a master's degree in human resources—correct?"

Employers are looking to see if you have three types of skills: content, functional (also known as transferable), and adaptive. Content skills involve knowledge that specifically pertains to work, such as computer programming and accounting. These are expressed as nouns. Functional skills describe how you interact with people, information, or things, and are expressed as verbs, such as organizing, managing, and communicating. Adaptive skills are personal attributes or characteristics stated as adjectives, such as being dependable, a team player, self-directed, or punctual.

Helpful Tips for Mastering the Behavioral-Based Interview:
- Examine your transferable skills and personal qualities required for the job.
- Review your resume and match your responses to those qualities and skills you included in it.
- Expound on your professional, volunteer, and educational experiences, briefly illustrating relevant skills and qualities.
- Use effective storytelling in your responses to capture your audience's attention.

Make sure you respond when applicable with a problem-answer-result (PAR) answer. You describe the problem, the action you took to solve the problem, and the positive results of those actions. Make sure to incorporate the requirements of the position you're interviewing for to convey that you are right for the job.

Telephone Interview
Many companies use telephone interviews to identify and recruit candidates for employment, or to screen candidates to narrow the pool of those who will be invited for a face-to-face interview. Telephone interviews save the company money when interviewing out-of-town candidates. In addition to being prepared for the scheduled telephone interview, you should be ready for a random, unexpected interview. You never know when a recruiter or a hiring manager might call and ask if you have a few minutes to talk about a job. If you are prepared, you will have an advantage over your competitors before the face-to-face interviews are conducted.

Tips for Mastering the Telephone Interview:
- Make sure you are available during the scheduled interview time.
- Ensure you are in a quiet, comfortable place where you will not be disturbed.
- Have your resume handy, as well as the questions you have prepared to ask the interviewer.

- If you have a mirror, place it in front of you and look at it as you speak. Make sure to smile throughout the interview, as it will make you sound more positive and optimistic.
- Be enthusiastic and speak professionally.
- Stand while you are talking. This helps your breathing intake and helps you to speak with distinction when articulating your words.
- Don't interrupt the interviewer when he or she is speaking.
- Make sure you have researched the company ahead of time; it pays to do your homework.
- If you have the opportunity, ask the interviewer about the position you are interviewing for. This will give good information and help you develop responses.

The Dining Interview

The purpose of the dining or luncheon interview is to assess how well you can handle yourself in a social setting. In this interview, follow the middle-ground rule. In other words, order meals that are within the middle-price range. Avoid wine or alcohol even if others are drinking. If asked, simply say, "No thank you." This conveys to those around you that you value making sound decisions.

Helpful Tips for Mastering the Dining Interview:
- Let the interviewer lead. He or she is the host, and you are the guest.
- Do not sit until your host does.
- Choose food that is not sticky or prone to stain.

- Do not begin eating until your interviewer eats.
- If the interviewer orders coffee and dessert, join them. It is polite; do not leave them eating alone.
- If your interviewer wants to talk business, do so. If not, wait for the right moment to bring up business topics.
- If you tend to get food stuck in your teeth, excuse yourself from the table for a moment to check yourself in the mirror.
- Practice eating and conversing simultaneously.
- Thank your interviewer for the meal.

The Performance/Audition Style Interview

The audition interview style is a unique process in which the interviewer takes the job seeker through a simulation or brief exercise in order to assess their skills. This style can be used for employers who want to see the candidate in action before they make their decision, such as the military or companies looking to hire computer programmers or trainers. This style is especially beneficial to candidates, because it gives them the opportunity to demonstrate their abilities while also giving them a sense of the job.

Sample Interview Questions

All interview styles share questions in common, such as the ones below.

1. What are you looking for in a technical company like ours? (Here the interviewer is trying to determine if you

are going to stay, or just learn the job and then leave for a different opportunity.)

- ▸ Answer: I believe my technical skills would be an asset to your organization, and I welcome the opportunity to be a vital part and a committed team member of your fine institution.

2. What skills can you bring to this company?
   - ▸ Answer: I've always been interested in this type of business. And, after researching your firm, I believe my strategic, technical, organizational, and leadership skills would be very valuable to your company. If afforded the opportunity to be a part of your company, my experience will speak for itself.

3. Why did you leave your last job?
   - ▸ Answer: I liked it, but I feel I'll have more challenges and opportunities here.

4. What are your strengths and weaknesses? (Note: The recruiter doesn't really want to hear about your weaknesses, so don't give them any.)
   - ▸ Answer: I am honest, reliable, and conscientious. My weakness is that I am considered too conscientious by my friends. Some call me a workaholic. (If you are applying for a job where you will be handling money, emphasize that you are careful and accurate. For example, mention that you balance your checkbook to the penny.)

5. What are your favorite pastimes?
    - Answer: I like reading, traveling, swimming, bowling, and tennis. (Sports or any energetic activities are good, because they give the recruiter the idea that you are enthusiastic and competitive.)

Note: Please keep in mind that these are sample questions to give you a feel for what the interviewer is looking for. You should not say anything you can't back up.

Additional Interview Questions:

- Tell me about yourself.
- What kind of work interests you?
- Are you willing to travel?
- Are you willing to work overtime?
- What have you learned from your jobs or internships?
- Why do you want to work here?
- What did you like/dislike about your last job?
- How long are you planning to stay with the company?
- Tell me about your greatest accomplishments.
- How well do you work under pressure?
- What interests you most about this job?
- What can you do for us that someone else can't do?
- Tell me about a challenging problem you have had to deal with.
- What do you do when you are faced with problems or stresses at work?
- Describe an important goal you've set and your success in meeting it.

- How do you approach tasks that you dislike or that are uninteresting to you?
- Tell me about a time when you had to use verbal communication skills in order to get a point across that was important to you.
- Tell me about an experience in which you had to speak up and tell other people what you thought.
- Give me an example of a clever way you motivated your coworkers or subordinates.
- What types of decisions have you made without consulting your boss?
- Describe how you have overcome a job-related obstacle.
- Give me an example of a time when you used your fact-finding skills to gain information needed to solve a problem; then tell me how you analyzed the information and came to a decision.
- Describe the most significant written document, report, or presentation that you've created.
- Give me an example of a time when you were able to communicate successfully with a coworker, even when that person may not have liked you.
- What do you expect from a supervisor?

Follow-Up

Remember that your work is not done when the interview ends. In most cases, you can't simply sit back and wait for the job offer. Instead, you must follow up with your potential employer. If your follow-up is effective, you will appear professional and polite. Follow-ups are too important to dismiss.

Be proactive and consider the follow-up a strategic part of your job search process. It can give you the advantage you need to get the job offer over other candidates who interviewed for the position. Use these techniques to show your continued interest in the job, but don't convey desperation.

There are many ways you can follow up with a prospective employer, but the most effective and lasting approach is with an email.

Helpful Tips for Writing Thank-You Emails and Notes:
- Address the email or note to a specific person.
- When writing a follow-up email or note, be sure you have the correct titles and names of all the people who interviewed you.
- If more than one person interviewed you, send a separate email or note to each person.
- Send the email or note as soon as possible after your interview, preferably the same day or next day.
- Even if you were turned down for the job, use the thank-you email or note to express your appreciation for being considered and your interest in future opportunities.
- Get in the habit of writing thank-you notes after every interview. You never know what opportunities will arise from this kind gesture.

Post-Interview Tips
- Alert your references ahead of time that they may be getting a phone call from your prospective employer.

- Continue your job search, even if you feel confident that you will be offered a position.
- You can follow up with a telephone call to the employer within a week to ten days if you have not received notice the job was filled.
- Be patient. Sometimes the hiring process takes longer than the employer expects.
- Maintain a good rapport with the company you are planning to leave in case you do not get a job offer.

Sample Thank-You Letter

Dear Addressee:
Thank you for the opportunity to discuss the secretarial position this morning. Our conversation gave me a better understanding of ABC Company and the job requirements. The additional information from Max and Kathryn was helpful in gaining a deeper understanding of the position.

My strong office and interpersonal skills will enable me to make a contribution to your company. I am proficient in all the computer software packages you use and have the customer service experience you seek.

I enjoyed meeting the office staff and touring the facility. Your company is clearly a quality organization with an emphasis on efficiency and a dedication to teamwork. I would consider it a privilege to join your team and look forward to hearing from you.

Again, thank you for your time and consideration.

Sincerely,

You
2233 Anytime Street
Anywhere, KS 55555
(000) 505–5555

Sample Thank-You Note #1

Date

Dear Addressee,

Thank you for interviewing with me for the accountant position today. I appreciate the information you shared and enjoyed meeting Ms. Smith from the Accounting Department.

My interest in working for Lund Industries is stronger than ever, and based on your description of the position, I know I can do a good job.

I will contact you by Tuesday of next week to learn of your decision. Again, thank you for your time and consideration.

Sincerely,

You

Sample Thank-You Note #2

Date

Dear Addressee,
Thank you for taking the time to discuss the accounting position with me. It was a pleasure meeting you and the other panel members.

OPTASIA Industries sounds like the perfect place for me to use my skills, especially since you use the WXY system. It is the same system I have been supporting the past three years. My proven track record and accomplishments with cost-effective systems can be an asset to your company.

Again, thank you for your consideration. I look forward to hearing from you and to the possibility of joining your staff.

Sincerely,

You

STEP VI—SECURING THE DEAL

The Job Offer
Evaluating the Job Offer

> *"If any of you lack wisdom, let him ask of God, that giveth to all men liberally, and upbraideth not; and it shall be given him."*
> —James 1:5 KJV

You have completed the interviewing process. You should commend yourself for your hard work and for presenting yourself as a strong candidate. You have followed the principles of this book and have done everything possible to impress your potential employer.

And then—you've been offered the job! Success! That's more great news to celebrate. No more sweating bullets; you've arrived.

So, what should you do now? Should you accept the job offer? If so, should you accept the salary package as is, or should you negotiate for better terms? Indeed, these are pertinent questions that you must ask yourself before taking the plunge. Only you can decide what is best for you.

When you are caught up in the excitement of getting what you wanted, it's more important than ever to keep a level head and exercise sound judgment. Remember: Your chief aim throughout this process has been to obtain the job you sought with a solid company. Make sure you are equipped with the information you need to make a decision that benefits you and your employer. To be misinformed and to take a position with a company for the wrong reasons could leave you dissatisfied and wanting more from a company and your career. On the other hand, after you have gathered your facts and weighed the pros and cons, if the scale leans heavily toward accepting the position, go for it! I am rooting for you.

Remember: This phase of the job search process is as crucial as the others. To be successful, you must do two things: Assess the company using the information you have gathered before, during, and after the interview; and assess the salary package offered to you.

Assessing/Evaluating a Company's Culture
You should have been learning about the company throughout the job search process, but the interview has given you a new perspective that will help you process the information you have learned as well as search for more. Now that you have

been offered a job, it's crucial that you examine or reexamine the company's goals, strategies, and plans. Ask yourself if the company has a concise mission statement that establishes objectives for management, employees, stockholders, and even partners. You must be able to see eye-to-eye with the company's mission, or at least be willing to work with its strategic plan. If you are not comfortable with what you learn, then you should be wary of accepting the offer.

Examine every aspect of the company's culture. Study the management team, which is the glue that holds everything together. Identify the goals management has set for the company. A company with a strong management team has resilience and tenacity (just look at Berkshire Hathaway's record). Examine the length of tenure for the CEOs and other upper-level management officials, which can tell you in what direction the company is going and how much stability it has. For instance, General Electric's former CEO, Jack Welch, was with the company for two decades, and many proclaimed him one of the best managers of all time.

If you have not already done so, research the company to see if it is financially sound. Make sure it is not facing a major lawsuit or shouldering an astronomical debt. The last thing you need is to accept a position with a company that goes belly-up. Look at its financial results—preferably each quarter to determine its stability.

Unfortunately, there are no clear and concise guidelines set in stone as to assessing a company's culture before accepting a job offer. Many of these aspects are intangible. Ultimately, you should work where you want, even if not everything on the balance sheet adds up. Regardless, the principles of this chapter should help you make your decision.

Assessing the Salary

When you are offered a job, let your potential employer broach the salary issue first. Depending on the circumstances, the salary may be negotiable, and if it is, you should give yourself an opportunity to make a good job offer even better. If the idea of negotiating makes you uncomfortable, think how annoyed you will feel upon learning that a coworker hired at the same time and performing the same duties as you is making more money because he or she negotiated, and you didn't. If you and the company can't come to an agreement, then you may have to ask yourself the tough question: Should I take it or leave it?

As in other areas of your job search, effective negotiation begins with effective preparation. You should have a price range in mind before walking in the door. Often, a company will mention a salary range during the interviewing process, but if it doesn't, a few hours of research could earn you thousands of dollars. Websites such as www.salary.com, www.payscale.com, and www.livecareer.com/salary provide estimates for salaries that are appropriate for your education and skills in your geographical location. Or take advantage of the internet and browse your digital library business resource tools and research journals and other helpful resources that can provide you with a salary range for the position you are seeking.

When you have researched your salary options and assessed your situation, you should settle on three distinct salary ranges: a top salary that is the best you could expect, a middle salary that would be a reasonable compromise and a win-win for you and your employer, and a bottom salary you could live with while you prove yourself to the company.

Handling Negotiations

Never appear to be indecisive or nervous. Handy meditation and breathing tips can be lifesavers. Five minutes of meditation can sharpen your mind, rejuvenate your senses; thus, giving you a more peaceful persona. Demonstrate confidence: Stand straight, look forward, speak slowly and clearly. Let your persona convey success. When others see confidence in you, they will respect and reciprocate it. Remember, you want the prospective employer to believe he or she is getting a priceless jewel—you! Stick to your guns but be willing to compromise if necessary.

Face-to-Face

If you are interviewed and offered the job on the spot, be prepared to negotiate on the spot. Therefore, it is important to research your salary range (and the company) ahead of time. This situation can work to your advantage because it lets you know that the employer likes you, and if you play your cards right and have done your homework, then you might leave the table with the job in the bag. When faced with an on-the-spot job offer, remember three important points:

- Be polite and thank the interviewer for the offer. Let the interviewer know you are interested in the position. If you have changed your mind, share this information in a timely manner and demonstrate that you are considerate of others' time. You may want to apply for a position with the company in the future and your thoughtfulness will likely be remembered.
- If money has been discussed (by the interviewer first), suggest a salary range. This gives you room to compromise rather than being locked into a definite amount that can prompt the interviewer to withdraw the offer.
- If at some point during the discussion you and the interviewer cannot reach an agreement, be polite and ask if you can think about the offer overnight and call the next day with your answer. Keep your word and call back promptly. It is important to quickly notify a hiring manager of your decision, and if you wish to negotiate further issues, you should do it at once.

Responding in Writing to a Job Offer

You may want to confirm in writing the position you were offered. Make sure that you know for certain in what department you will be placed. You do not want to accept the job and then find yourself in another position when you report for work.

Some companies require that you respond to their offer in writing. If so, make sure you respond via email by their deadline. A delay can mean forfeiture of a position and will make it more difficult to apply to that company in the future. If you have concerns, be sure to express them in a clear and concise manner. This gives the hiring manager a chance to evaluate your ideas and possibly discuss them with decision-makers to make a counter-offer.

Use the Following Guidelines for Writing a Negotiating Letter:
- Be positive and leave room for further discussions.
- Make sure your letter is factual on all points discussed.
- Thank the organization for its interest in you and express your interest in the organization.
- List your concerns along with suggestions and be open to feedback.
- Convey in your letter that you are confident that a positive agreement can be reached.
- Compose your letter, critique it, and email it within two to three hours of the job offer.

Sample Negotiation Letter for a Job Offer

7524 Anytime Manor
Cloverdale, AR 12578
(555) 111–2345
Add email here

Date

Dear:

Thank you for offering me the position as Customer Relations Executive of the Accounting Department. I appreciate your confidence in my skills and want to assure you that I will do my best to contribute to your business objectives. I am most interested in working for your company, and I look forward to contributing to it.

As we discussed, based on my qualifications, work experience, and market value, I am looking for a starting salary in the $35,000-$40,000 range. Can we explore the possibility of raising the salary offer to $37,500 from the initial offer of $34,000 after six months of successful performance in the position?

I am confident that we can reach a mutual agreement. If there are no objections, I will call Friday morning and schedule an appointment to discuss the issue and the criteria for a successful performance in the position.

Thank you for the job offer. I look forward to meeting with you again and to joining your company.

Sincerely,
You

Sample Job Offer Response Letter

7524 Anytime Manor
Cloverdale, AR 12578
(555) 111-2345
Add email here

Date

Dear:

I am very pleased to accept the job offer for the Administration Manager position. I appreciate your confidence in my skills. I am eager to join the team at (company name).

I have submitted my resignation to my employer today and, as agreed, my first day with your company will be July 8, 2020. Per your request, I have signed and enclosed the offer letter.

Again, thank you for providing me with this opportunity. I look forward to fulfilling your expectations.

Sincerely,
You

Conclusion

Success in life depends on a simple formula: *wise thoughts + wise planning = wise, informed decisions.* It's true regarding your career goals and your personal life. It works whether you are negotiating a salary or finding a mate.

Every moment is a new opportunity to start making wise decisions, and every day is a chance to create a new vision for you. Accept this and you can face life optimistically, you can overcome the challenges that have defeated you, and you can prepare yourself for change, because change is inevitably coming.

Remember: Failure is never final. If you have missed the mark in any area of life, forgive yourself and move on. If you have recently landed a job that is less than the job of your dreams, or if you find yourself earning less than the salary you deserve because you didn't know how to negotiate, don't fret! Instead, apply the six steps and prepare for a new life. It's not an accident that you received this book.

Don't simply read about the six steps. Study and learn them so that you'll be ready for your next career move or salary negotiation. Keep this book on a special shelf—your "arsenal of knowledge shelf"—so that it will be easy to retrieve when you need it. Know that your work and preparation will pay off—if not now, then later. Success awaits you. Go forth and claim what is already yours.

I wrote this book with you in mind. I wrote it to give you an extra advantage to help you excel. Don't hesitate. Do what others like you are doing. Apply this knowledge and see your destiny manifest itself. Know that I am rooting for you. You can achieve what you believe!

PART 2

Master Your Move;
Mind Your Own Business

STEP VII—MASTER YOUR MOVE

Mind Your Own Business

"Whether therefore ye eat, or drink, or whatsoever ye do, do all to the glory of God."

—1 Corinthians 10:31 KJV

*H*ave *you ever played a game of chess?* If you have, you know that you must think several moves ahead before making your next move to achieve your goal—winning! Achieving success in the entrepreneurial realm is similar.

I have watched countless talented, skilled people deprive themselves of the opportunity to become entrepreneurs and start their own businesses. Some have held back on their dreams of starting their own business because of misguided notions or ideas that to make six figures or to be successful, one must have a college degree. Although having a college degree is commendable, it is not the sole key to success or to achieving six figures. I know successful and prosperous businesspeople who do not have a college degree and have excelled in running their own business.

Master Your Move
I encourage you if you have a strong passion or drive and know your talents and skills can be used by others, to pay attention to the voice inside you (inner man that your Creator speaks to) and start your own business. You possess something valuable that can benefit others. Release the entrepreneur within you!

If that leap of faith seems too risky, consider a gradual launch; start a part-time pursuit into the entrepreneurial realm. Or, if you are close to retirement and want to continue working, consider working for yourself. Make your talents and skills you have acquired or perfected work for you. Remember: You are the expert or master of your destiny. Rule in this realm that you were placed.

While considering my suggestion and exploring the idea of being your own boss, ask yourself: Where do I fit in making my business a success? I am willing to bet—anywhere you please. You must believe in yourself. Be determined, stay focused, and learn your craft. Always be willing to learn from others' successes and failures (in your current job or from your competitors). Learning from others' success or misfortune can help you to strategically focus so you can navigate around any pitfalls that could be future obstacles.

Do What You Love, the Money Will Come

You have the advantage; you have a talent or skill yearning to be applied to helping or serving others. Think about something you are interested in starting or learning, or something you are already good at. It can be something that requires little effort to you or entails less competition. If this talent or skill you want to expand or offer to others is something you really enjoy, it won't seem like work. You would reap the benefits of being paid for providing a service you love.

There are advantages to having your own business—extra streams of income, meeting new customers (that can develop into professional and personal relationships), and strengthening or sharpening your talents or skills, and much more. My philosophy is: Do what you love; the money or perks will follow.

If you are knowledgeable in the areas of real estate, cooking or catering food, traveling, pet training, etc., then learn the skills or techniques that will enable you to start a business in your area of interest; become an expert.

Mind Your Own Business

When minding your own business and considering budget factors, I would recommend doing as much as you can yourself and seeking professional expertise in the areas in which you lack knowledge. The advantage here is you will save hundreds of dollars, better understand your company, and have less need to consult with a lawyer or tax consultant every time you have a legal or tax question.

If you start a small, part-time business to build experience and a client base, you will eventually reach the point where you must consider incorporating. This is something too often required in your entrepreneurial venture. If you decide to incorporate, you can download the business corporation forms and instructions for your appropriate state and complete them yourself. If you are unclear on the specifics of completing the forms, you can call your state corporation commission for assistance. You can speak with a professional who can answer your questions about completing the forms. If necessary, you can always contact an attorney to assist you with necessary information you need, or to review forms you completed. The same is true for tax forms.

Consider the tax advantages of having your own enterprise. If you have no employees, then you would not gain the liability protection that a corporation affords. On the other hand, if you do have employees, you may consider incorporating to protect yourself from potential negligence.

Incorporating, however, will not necessarily protect you from your own possible mishap or error. For example, if you injure someone in an accident on your way to a business meeting or running an errand, you would be personally liable. So, I would suggest buying business liability insurance. You can ask an insurance agent or a tax professional for more details. As you are establishing your business venture, I would recommend buying coverage of at least $1 million to protect yourself. The premium cost is reasonable, and the higher coverage can generally be extended to your automobile or homeowner's insurance policy at no extra charge. Again, ask or consult with a professional consultant about an umbrella liability policy.

Do the legwork and fill out as much as you can, and have a financial expert review your forms for accuracy. Taking the initiative and learning the foundation of your business affairs helps you better understand the processes and lifeline of your business. Remember: Knowledge is power; the more you know about your business, the more control you maintain over your own affairs. This results in less stress and more flexibility.

What You Need to Succeed as an Entrepreneur

There are many elements for succeeding in business. Three important elements are: knowledge, talent or skills, and having the right attitude. Let's look at each of these prerequisites in further detail.

Use Your Tools to Become an Expert

Tool #1 Knowledge (Needed for Entrepreneurs):

Position yourself to become an expert in your field. If you think you don't know enough about your subject area or industry, do what I did: Go to the library, take training courses, earn certifications or licenses, and ask experts for mentorship. This is an effective strategy for sharpening the tools in your arsenal.

One way of researching or finding experts that can assist you in learning more about your industry or field is to seek out associations (For example: The Guide to National Professional Certification Programs; third edition, Philip M. Harris) or networks dedicated to your subject matter, field, or related industry. Indeed, that would be a good starting point for finding an association or network that can provide valuable information regarding your industry trade or profession.

Mental Training; Make It Work for You
Albert Einstein, widely considered the epitome of intelligence, stressed the importance of challenging your brain and training your mind to develop mental skills and abilities. The fact that Einstein valued knowledge was evident in his research. We can learn from his eternal quest for knowledge; we should use this same passion or drive for knowledge to stay ahead of the game in business.

The idea of starting a business is like a bag of seed. Executing the plan and running a business is like planting and tending to seed in the ground. If all goes well, you will reap the harvest and share the benefits with others. If you are hesitant or indecisive about being a business owner, trust me, the benefits exceed the apprehensiveness you may be feeling. Be open to new and useful knowledge; it will propel your business to heights you could have only dreamed of. This boosts your confidence as others reap the rewards of your successful product or services. So, embrace knowledge and pursue it. It is the jewel of your business.

You Can't Afford Not to Seek Knowledge

Knowledge is the foundation that your business or prospective business needs to succeed. Thinking that courses or trainings are too expensive can cause you to forfeit opportunities that would be beneficial. If you are financially challenged, don't allow that obstacle to interfere with your destiny.

If a course or a training opportunity seems too expensive, I would encourage you to assess the opportunity, strategize, seek similar opportunities, and compare pricing. I have sought training that I perceived was a bit steep for my budget. I didn't let that challenge cloud my creative thinking. I put my thinking cap on and explored ways to make the training happen.

I even reached out to a training vendor and asked about payment plans. I was able to get a payment option to pay half down and pay the remaining half before I attended the training. This was a big break for me because the certification was invaluable to my business. It was a priceless investment in myself and my business.

Remember: There is more than one way to achieve a goal. You must think creatively to find solutions to any given problem. Explore options. Be creative with your resources as you seek knowledge. It's an investment in yourself and your business. Trust me, it will pay off tremendously as you seek to widen your knowledge base. Act with courage and stay committed to succeeding. I am confident you will if you put forth the effort and persevere through any challenges that may arise.

What Knowledge Can Do for You

Einstein said, "Education is what remains after one has forgotten what one has learned in school." When you expand your knowledge base, you can far exceed your classroom learning. You gain a distinct advantage and soar above those challenged to think creatively. Going the extra mile to conquer your quest for knowledge shows that you value learning and the success of your entrepreneurial venture. For example, if your enterprise was conceived in the early 1980s, you would now need to launch new technology and social media projects for the strategic and competitive positioning of your company because social media didn't exist in the 1980s.

The tireless pursuit of knowledge helps you secure your seat at the table. Develop a knowledge strategy and examine it often. This will allow you to keep up with fresh ideas and information that will be valuable to you and your business venture for years to come. In short, attaining knowledge is a significant competitive strategy. Stay ahead of the game.

Tool #2 Talent or Skills (Needed for Entrepreneurs)
Every person has a talent or skill to offer others, which can be used for profit and nonprofit ventures. A talent is an inborn quality, whereas a skill is something that can be developed and perfected with practice. Entrepreneurship is a skill that is practiced and perfected by those who are committed to their passion or goal of developing a product or service to better humanity.

Make Your Talents and Skills Work for You

How do you make your talent and skills work for you? By positioning yourself, planning, and having courage, commitment, and confidence in what you do.

So, if you are, indeed, someone who wants to launch your enterprise, but unsure where to start, do a self-reflection or a self-inventory; explore your talents and skills. You can define your business by focusing on the undertaking you wish to pursue—that business product or service you would like to offer to the world and make a living. This will be the mission of your business. More detail of the Self-SWOT Analysis is provided in Step V of this book (See: Put Your Best Foot Forward; The Interview for Self-SWOT Analysis Exercise).

According to Proverbs 18:6, a man's gifts will make room for him. How do you know if your talents and skills are working for you after you began to pursue your enterprise? First, you should define your goal for achieving success as it relates to your talents and skills. What do you want to do? Achieving the indicators below is a sign your talents and skills are working for you. Your persistence and commitment to your business will determine the longevity.

Indicators That Your Talents and Skills are Working for You:
Questions to ask yourself:

1. Will my talents and skills bring me success?

2. Will I be able to reap positive benefits, including financial, from my talents and skills?

3. Will my talents and skills bring me exposure as an expert—publicity or fame?

4. Will my talents and skills bring a sense of fulfillment for me and others who reap the benefits of my talents and skills?

Tool #3: Right Attitudes (Needed for Entrepreneurs):
Having the right attitude can change and enhance your life. Your strategic mindset toward entrepreneurship as it relates to your mission in establishing an enterprise, or improving an existing business, can be a game changer for you.

Five "P" Attitudes of the Business World
When reflecting on the significance of attitudes needed to succeed in the entrepreneurial world, five distinctive "P" factors come to mind—passion, perfecting, practice, persistence, and patience.

First, passion is the fire or fuel that drives your business success. Second, you must strive to perfect your talents and skills and hone your expertise. Having an attitude of perfecting motivates you to make your business the best it can be. Focusing on continuous improvement will keep you on your toes and going the extra mile. You will seek out opportunities to learn and grow in life and business. Others will notice your mindset and will be drawn to you. Third, practice is the can-do attitude and behavior to execute. With this attitude, you will sharpen and define your talents and skills. You have heard the saying, "practice makes perfect." Apply this trait and you will write your own ticket and soar above the stars!

Fourth, persistence allows you to keep going when all else seems impossible. With persistence, you are like the Energizer Bunny; you keep going, and going, and going. Importantly, a persistent attitude is needed to get you out of the valleys you may encounter and help you climb mountains. Lastly, patience is necessary. Plant a seed and cultivate your passion, perfecting (maturing), persistence (continual), practice, and patience. See your business thrive.

> Who looks outside, dreams; who looks inside, awakens."
> —Carl Jung

© Copyright by Lauri Williams 2009

Explore "P" Attitudes of the Business World

As an author, trainer, coach, and entrepreneur, I can attest to the positive outcomes I have seen in applying or using the "P" Attitudes in business and life. Keep an open mind and get acquainted with incorporating the "P" Attitudes and see how these qualities can work for you. I am certain that you may already be employing some if not all of them.

My philosophy is: "My Success Brings You Success!" As I attentively employed the "P" Attitudes when coaching my clients, I saw outstanding results. My fame and the wave of publicity I received as an author and entrepreneur brought success to my clients as well. The "P" Attitude of passion for succeeding motivated me, and that same mindset transferred to my clients. They could see my genuine desire to see them succeed. One client said to me that my passionate attitude to see her succeed encouraged her to look within herself and fueled the fire to fulfill her purpose—to write and publish her first book. She has since written and published two books. I assisted her with gaining television media attention. She is motivated and contemplating writing her third book.

You can achieve amazing results when applying the "P" Attitudes. My successful results have created a high demand for my time and service. The good news is as your success rate grows, so does your income, reputation, reference list, and client base. I consistently apply passion, perfecting, practice, persistence, and patience attitude factors when working with clients.

Further, I want to encourage you by saying that you can achieve your purpose just as I and so many other people have with the "P" Attitudes. Just imagine what you will be able to do when you employ these invaluable strategies in your life and your business.

Three "C" Attitudes of Business

Starting a business can seem overwhelming—in fact, there's so much to do and to figure out. Where do you find customers, how do you secure financing, and where do you locate your business? All this may seem terrifying. I know because I have been there. By applying the Three "C" Attitudes—courage, commitment, and confidence, you can achieve things beyond your wildest dreams.

Courage

It takes courage to take the first step—to start and operate your own business. I want to let you know you can do it. You can succeed. You will succeed! Stay motivated and get energized. Be the Energizer Bunny. Commit to infusing the planning and execution of your business with fun. This will lessen the tension.

Courage requires one to employ a strategic focus in life as it relates to attaining that comfortable and well-paying business you long to have. A strategy I recommend is the Self-SWOT Analysis (covered in Step V: Putting Your Best Foot Forward-The Interview). In this exercise you can examine your SWOT—strength, weaknesses, opportunities, and threats.

Threats as it relates to the business environment and yourself. This evaluative tool can shed light on your real perspectives and help you see where you should focus your attention to get ahead. I recommend trying this exercise at least once a year to help you stay in tune with yourself and your business so you can grow and prosper.

© Copyright by Lauri Williams 2009

Commitment

The next "C" Attitude is commitment. Commitment is essential to business. It is a mindset in which you are dedicated to something or someone. In this case, you are dedicated to your business. It is the pledge you make to yourself that through thick or thin you will stick with your endeavor because you know and believe in its value and the impact it has on others.

And regardless of the difficulties you encounter, your talents and skills will help you succeed. Until you can fully commit to your business, you will lack effectiveness.

Confidence

You must first believe that you can be successful and look within for your talents and skills and manifest success in your life and your business. Success is yours for the taking. Believe it!

Confidence can be felt and demonstrated. Confidence is vital to gaining the support of customers and helpful in putting you ahead of your competitors. This characteristic should not be taken lightly. Conduct yourself with the right amount of confidence and you will be a winner!

If you have a specific talent, skill, or service that very few can offer, potential customers will buy and keep buying from you. You must demonstrate that confidence as it helps to promote you and your talent, skill, or service of your business. Start showing your confidence in yourself as it will help develop your strategic position in your market or industry.

We all have low moments at times; it's only normal. If you feel you are lacking confidence, one tip I have learned is to act as if you have confidence. In other words, if you project confidence, even if you don't initially feel that way, you will begin to feel confident. It works like a charm!

Sometimes circumstances or situations hinder our enthusiasm and flow, but it's important to remain strong and committed so you can succeed, both for yourself and others. Stay true to your business's mission and purpose. You have something valuable to offer.

Three "C" Attitudes Bring Success

I have taught success principles for many years. I have trained and mentored many people from various backgrounds in pursuing and attaining their goals and fulfilling their purpose in business and life. The countless testimonials I receive from my clients make me more committed and confident in serving my clients with sincerity and professionalism. A previous client of mine, who is a blind, disabled veteran, shared that my coaching and mentoring helped pull him out of a pit of despair and look within to see the talents and skills he could offer to others; he decided to pursue his passion and let his talents and skills work for him. Thus, my client went on to graduate from a school for the blind and learned to read braille. He also acquired computer skills. My client is a motivational speaker and author who travels the world encouraging others with disabilities and teaching them to be winning warriors—to overcome challenges in life with courage, commitment, and confidence and to believe in themselves.

Also, another client, who discovered her writing and speaking abilities in her late 60s, achieved her goals. Her decision to become a business owner after retiring from teaching was a courageous one. She wanted to work for herself but was unsure where to start. So, she decided to work with me. We established an agreement, and I developed a distinct plan for her. She committed to following the plan and achieved success in her life.

I coached my client and provided effective tools and helped her to explore her Self-SWOT Analysis. Afterward my client was certain that she wanted to pursue writing and speaking. She took a leap of faith and did something she had only dreamed of for years. She became a professional speaker and author.

The results were amazing. She has traveled on a cruise to the Bahamas and traveled to Europe promoting her book. She has received media recognition too. Also, she now writes a weekly article for her local newspaper. These exciting ventures my client attributes to adopting the "C" Attitudes of business:

- Courage to step out and do what she had only dreamed of doing despite uncertainty

- Commitment to fulfilling her purpose, both for herself and others she has inspired
- Confidence in herself and making her talents and skills work for her and helping to encourage others

Three Rs of Business

Performance indicators are crucial to any business professional. The more awareness you have of how performance indicators work, the more comfortable you will be in steering your enterprise to success. It will be an unforgettable journey. Allow the indicators—results, reputation, and rates—to work for you and you will soar with the Three Rs of Business.

Results

Results are indicators of success, that can be positive or negative, by which you gauge your performance. Results are also the very thing that customers look for in a product or service. Make every effort to deliver with excellence. If you are doing what you love with passion and pride, the results will extend to your business partners and supporters.

Remember customers are drawn to a product or service that will fulfill their needs.

Developing your talents and skills and making consistent efforts to gain knowledge can produce tremendous results. As stated earlier, as you become more successful, you will boost your income, enhance your reputation, and grow your reference list or client base.

Reputation

Customers are attracted to what works and they are inclined to patronize a business that has an outstanding reputation and offers products and services that meet their needs.

Remember that your reputation, comprised of your talents and services, is the sustenance of your business.

Moreover, a good reputation means that many have utilized your products or services and found them to yield positive results. So, let the positive name or fame of your business work in your favor. A good standing in the public eye will lead to opportunities for building good rapport and professional relationships in your network.

An increased network base means you have an extended reference pool of people that can market you or your business. Thus, more people who will spread the word about your business, in turn, can increase the number of people in your network database. This can give your business a competitive stance among your competitors.

Rates

So, what do six-figure earnings look like for a talented, skilled entrepreneur? How can one go about and set a goal to attain this after opening the doors? There are certain factors you need to consider, like your working hours. Deciding working hours and rate of pay can give you an initial estimate for setting goals to achieve the six-figure mark.

To illustrate, a talented, skilled entrepreneur whose passion and purpose is photography can easily achieve six figures. If a photographer were able to secure clientele and schedule fifteen sessions a week at $150 per appointment, her weekly income would be around $2,200.

Keep in mind that you want to pursue what you have passion for and perfect your talents or skills. Then doing what you love won't seem like work. The passion you put into it will be rewarding, and as you consistently build and perfect your craft, many will come near and far to employ your services.

In order to determine your rate of pay, you must first understand the value of your talents and skill in the marketplace. This is crucial. To determine the value of your talents and skills, you must demonstrate uniqueness from your competitors—show how you surpass those in the local or national market or industry.

In building your skills and establishing yourself as an expert, pursuing knowledge helps you write your own ticket. Positioning yourself as an expert allows you to be in the know. This gives you the knowledge to help your prospective clients as it improves your competitive edge in business. Make sure you are attentive of this helpful information; it will pay off if you do.

Part 3

Six Steps Six Figures
A Power-Packed Guide for Your Career Goals
and Life God's Way

Second Edition
Updated & Expanded

STEP VIII—MASTERING YOUR MOVE

Incorporating FAME In Your Life

> *"What doth it profit, my brethren, though a man say he hath faith, and have not works? Can faith save him?*
>
> —James 2:14 KJV

Begin your journey; manifest your success today. I encourage you to incorporate the FAME principle in your life; take total control of your life and thoughts in every way. See yourself achieve your goals as you increase your level of success for you and others. You must understand it will require you to change your thinking as you take the steps needed to achieve your destiny. Success requires you to possess faith, take action, and move beyond your comfort zone. But know that success for you is attainable. You can achieve career success or establish an entrepreneurial empire. You can do it. There are no boundaries, except for those you set for yourself.

Know Your Purpose

You possess the talents and skills to achieve the successful lifestyle you desire. Position yourself with purpose to take the journey to get you there. All you need is a little help and encouragement in developing and accessing the power within you. Guess what? This book can encourage, enlighten, and motivate you, as it has countless others, to look within to succeed.

You may have heard the term "success" used in different ways. The dictionary defines success as attainment of one's aim, wealth, or fame, etc., but I believe success is the outward product of those elements listed. I believe success is knowing and living your true purpose in life. You can't move forward in peace if you are miserable not living in your purpose.

Succeed on Purpose

So, again, true success is knowing and living your life's purpose. That goes for your career goals and your own business. Everyone was created with an ability, drive, and passion to succeed in some fashion. We all were given the power (energy or ability to change things in our sphere) to succeed. What you do with that power and your innate talents and skills will determine your level of success.

Dear Reader, you have the potential to achieve whatever you want in life. It doesn't matter who you are. It does, however, require faith, belief in yourself, passion, focus, strength, and courage through tough times. Seek knowledge and let your passion drive you. If you adopt the "P" and "C" Attitudes for business and life, things will change for the better for you.

Make FAME Work for You

On your path to success, make the FAME principles work for you. FAME is focus, affirm, meditate, and expect. Take hold of the FAME principles and apply them consistently; they can gauge or measure the course of success in your life.

The FAME principles work if you discipline your thoughts and focus on accomplishing your goals and if you help others stay focused on their true purpose. Your success should bring others success. We were all created to reach our potential and to help others reach theirs.

FAME Principle #1 Focus

Focus, the first principle, is about having a strategy or plan and not allowing yourself to become distracted. In order to change your life, you must create a new vision for your life, and to do that, you must focus on the kind of success you want. By following the principles outlined in this book, you will be

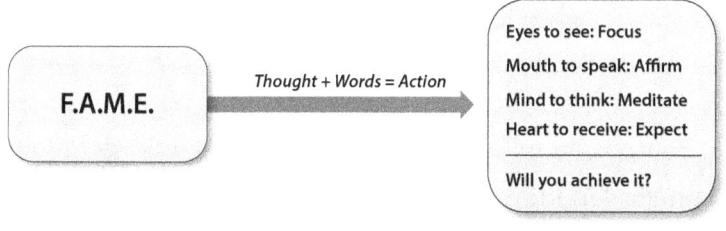

Lauri J. Williams

empowered to change your limiting beliefs and create powerful new beliefs that uplift you. But you must focus on your success. Real success comes from belief, thought, and faith. Remember this: Whatever a person can conceive in their heart or mind, they can manifest. A positive frame of mind will follow if you generate and maintain thoughts and beliefs, for the law of cause and effect is immutable. You are in the driver's seat.

© Copyright by Lauri Williams 2009

Your vision reflects how you see yourself; it is your dominant view in life and determines how you live. If you keep a positive view of your success—with clear and specific goals as to your level of success, you can prosper. You can have complete control over your outlook. By maintaining a clear picture in your mind and heart of where you want to be a year or two from now, you can align the forces you need to bring about the kind of success you desire for your life. And, dream big, because the size of your vision will determine the scope of your success.

On the other hand, if you let your doubts and fears—whether big or small—overwhelm you, it will undermine your success. You will manifest what you doubt and fear rather than the success you want and deserve. If you focus on the difficulties, problems, and negative people holding you back, you will get nowhere.

Remember this: You either create or block your success. If your vision is stronger than your doubts and fears, you will succeed. It's as simple as that.

Create a vision and then focus each day on the simple, concrete steps you've designed to make that vision a reality. Manifest what you want and intend to create in your life. You create what you are focusing on by concentrating on it with attention and awareness and keeping it in the back of your mind even when partaking in other activities. The emotions behind your thoughts determine the speed at which you manifest them.

Several years ago, the National Science Foundation revealed some very interesting information about a person's thoughts, stating that a person has an enormous number of thoughts a day. Deepak Chopra, author of *Quantum Healing,* and others maintain that people have anywhere from 12,000 to 65,000 thoughts per day. Thoughts cause emotions, and we can control those. Our emotions tell us what track we are on in life.

You must keep the big picture in mind, and not concern yourself with the intricate details, yet keep assuring yourself that you can and will achieve what you want. At times it may seem like you are your own coach and cheerleader, but you can be successful. I vividly recall how my outlook changed as I began to consistently focus on achieving success and my true purpose in life. Ten years ago, I went through a very emotionally and economically challenging career phase. I had been working hard for the wrong reasons, and I wasn't happy, because I felt I was not achieving my true success. I realized I was climbing a ladder of success that was leaning against the wrong building. Once I was able to acknowledge my feelings, set SMART goals, and remain focused, I released the author within me. I published the first edition of *Six Steps Six Figures: A Power-Packed Guide for Your Career Goals & Life God's Way*. I have received much recognition from that book as I traveled to various places promoting it. So, you see focusing moves you closer to living the reality that was once mere thoughts. It requires translating mental work into action, but it is attainable. Again, there may be periods when you feel like you are your own coach and cheerleader on your journey, but I can say this from experience—you can make it if you don't quit.

FAME Principle—Employ Your Own Wall Coach

Your desired success is welling up inside you and waiting to burst open and manifest itself in various forms. Success is the stuff we are made of, but not everyone realizes this. Why is that? Could it be that many that travel through this journey of life need a helping hand, a coach, a cheerleader to give them that spark of confidence to ignite courage to look within themselves?

If you need a little nudge of encouragement, you can create one. I call it the Wall Coach. It has really helped me when I am feeling low. It propelled me from simply scribbling wishful thoughts on notepads to becoming a professional consultant, speaker, and a published author.

© Copyright by Lauri Williams 2009

Making Your Own Wall Coach
What is a Wall Coach? It is a dry erase board or a poster board that you hang on your wall (this method is what helped me; each person can be creative to find inspiration and encouragement for themselves). Add colorful images of goals or dreams from different areas of your life that you want to turn into realities. For my Wall Coach, I started with five so that there would be one for each weekday, leaving Saturday and Sunday for me to reflect on the images. After my daily spiritual reading and meditation, I would visit my Wall Coach in the morning before I went to work and, in the evening, before I went to sleep until I achieved each of these goals.

Why was it so effective? Twice each day I faced myself on my terms and had an in-depth conversation with my higher self. I asked: What progress or steps did I make toward my goals, or did I waste another day? Meanwhile, it trained me to exercise my mind and to explore ways to achieve my desired goals. Psychologically it trained me to open my mind to see myself having what I wished for. At times I would find myself mentally drifting off to the success images on my wall, and a jolt of inspiration for new ways of achieving my goals would come to me. I would write down these nuggets of wisdom and draft a systematic plan to achieve those successes. Get into the habit of carrying a notepad with you.

If you are looking for extra encouragement, I would suggest creating your own Wall Coach. Remember, this is your Wall Coach, so be creative and make it relevant to your circumstances. Arrange your goals in the order of your level of desire for them. You can use photos from magazines, computer clip art, or whatever you choose. Do not clutter your wall. I chose five goals because I did not want to confuse my subconscious mind. You may want to start with just two or three. If your success focus is money, use photos and images of money instead of things you want to buy. Otherwise, you may get those things plus debt! I've found it helpful to use play money or play checks.

Don't tell anyone about your Wall Coach and certainly don't try to convince them of its effectiveness. If they are not supportive, it will only bring you down. Do not discount or let anyone else discount your dreams, goals, and success. Instead, let others see the changes in your life. If you are spiritual, place a symbol on your wall such as a Bible, a picture of Christ, scriptures, or other symbols of your faith. This gives your success a spiritual protection that opens a way for your Creator to work through you.

The Wall Coach can be valuable no matter your present circumstances, but it will not substitute for hard work and preparation. No matter how good their Wall Coaches are, it won't make average basketball players into NBA stars unless they are willing to sacrifice to improve. The same holds true for someone who is changing careers with no education or experience. Success requires focus, dedication, planning, believing in oneself, and carrying out established plans. Applying the Wall Coach can help you stay focused and accountable to yourself for achieving success.

You have the ingredients to be successful, but those ingredients will only sit in the pantry unless you stir them into a delicious dish. What are you making with your ingredients? How are you achieving success? Are you expecting others to create success for you? Remember: You determine your outcome! What will it be?

FAME Principle #2 Affirm

According to the first FAME principle, while you are focusing on your success, you also must affirm it. The tongue is small but powerful, and if it is used in the wrong way, it can be destructive.

Speak Your Destiny

Likewise, your tongue determines your destiny because the words you speak shape the life you live and the person you become. To be successful, you must focus on positive things and repeat daily positive affirmations about these things. An example affirming statement is, "I am prosperous and in good health," or, "Each day, I am getting better and better." Repeat these affirmations for 5 to 10 minutes daily, concentrating your attention on them much like you learned your multiplication tables as a child. Create the ones that feel right for you. When you repeat them, you firmly imprint them into your subconscious mind, so it accepts them as fact.

Repeat these affirmations for at least 21 days, just as you did with the Belief Power Exercise in chapter 2. Keep a journal of the way it changes your life. As with a seed, it takes time to grow. And, at times, it requires one to pull weeds—old, negative thoughts and ways of speaking. But by practicing consistency and patience, you will gain confidence, become more creative in your affirmations, and have incredible testimonies to share.

Don't Complain

One power-packed habit to incorporate into your life is simply to *stop* complaining. Be grateful and happy for the things you have. This will create a cycle of peace and order in your life. There will be times when challenges arise, but if you focus on being grateful and happy, you can crowd out those negative thoughts that cloud your mind.

Speak positively, and you will see your negative thoughts dissipate. Because you can't think about one subject and talk about another at the same time, your positive words will drown out your negative thoughts. You will program your mind to receive successful words, which will create successful thoughts that produce successful actions.

When we are trapped in a hole, we need a rope to climb out. Instead, too often we dig a deeper hole, and there is no more effective shovel than complaining. By complaining, we simply compound the negativity that has trapped us there in the first place. To overcome this, repeat positive affirmations such as, "I have the answer to this situation." You will eventually see your outlook change and realize that the circumstance is not as hopeless as you thought.

A Personal Experience
I am not different from you. I once faced intense financial hardship, and I chose to remain quiet and not complain. I decided that complaining wasn't working for me then and had never worked for me in the past. I remained quiet in my state, spoke positive affirmations about my financial affairs, and thanked God for the positive aspects of my life despite the debt I faced. The thought came to me, "Ask and speak with authority, hold your peace, don't complain, and I will give you the power." I followed those instructions, and it was as though a fresh new power sprang up from within me. I received the wisdom to get out of debt. I bought one of my dream cars at my price and on my terms. I negotiated various business deals to the mutual benefit of all involved. I was even very fortunate to meet an editor to edit my books.

Staying calm and not complaining has benefits for you and those around you. When negativity comes your way, it can seem challenging to control your tongue and not complain, but complaining only magnifies the negative. By remaining quiet and optimistic, you will see your situation from a broader perspective, and when that happens, you can accept what you can't change and begin working on what you can.

FAME Principle #3 Meditate

As Americans, we are programmed to act. Sometimes, the answer is just to be. That's the third part of the FAME principle: meditation. Meditation is a type of prayer or method for relaxation; it allows your inner self to let go of things that serve no purpose, while focusing your attention inward so you can find clarity and peace.

The practice of meditation is powerful and life-changing. It can help you discover your true purpose in life. I have found that meditation works whenever I am faced with a dilemma and need quick answers. It ignites untapped energy and gives me a fresh outlook on life.

How to Meditate

Meditation requires no exertion and no investment except time. Simply relax, sit still, and empty yourself. Silently reflect on a few meaningful words. As you contemplate these ideas, expand and move to action.

When meditating, concentrate on the outcome rather than the problem. When you sit still and separate yourself from the world around you, it is best not to think of failures.

If possible, let every care go while you focus. As you begin this daily practice, you will discover that some activities and daily demands are no longer necessary and that it is best to let them go rather than neglect your quiet time.

Meditation has physical benefits as well. It reduces your heart rate, blood pressure, and stress. It feeds you physically with a sense of bodily renewal, fresh energy, and well-being. It dissolves fatigue and tension. It quiets all nervousness, fear, oversensitivity, and the negativity of everyday life. Take it from me. Meditation has kept me intact when everything else was pulling me in other directions.

Maybe you are thinking: How will meditation or prayer produce tangible, satisfying, and successful results in my day-to-day affairs? When you meditate, you are dwelling on higher thoughts that carry you to a state of peace, realization, and illumination. Prayer takes you to a place of peace and focus as you connect with the heavenly creator or the ultimate supreme power. Prayer is that place you can tap into, the access to wisdom, and clarity to see what it is you're searching for. This sacred tool is a means to an end of getting the outcome you need and the supernatural assistance to make it on your entrepreneurial journey.

The best way for you to understand the significance of meditation and prayer is to try it for yourself. If you are one who spends most of your time being active, this will require discipline and practice, but it can be mastered. Soon you will understand and discover why meditation and prayer are the ultimate practices for mental clarity and discipline.

FAME Principle #4 Expect
EXPECT = DESIRE

The final part of the FAME principle is the most important: expecting. I believe that if you are a spiritual person who has discovered the workings of prayer, you can have a successful life. The simple formula is: Pray, then forgive (let go), and then expect (receive). Expecting involves some form of desire. If you do not desire, you don't expect, and the truth is everyone desires something. Negative people expect or desire negative things—perhaps so they can remain victims or receive attention.

Sowing and Reaping—(Doing and Expecting)
When you take action and apply yourself, you will succeed. It comes with believing in yourself, seeking wisdom, searching within yourself for the talents you have been given, applying them consistently, and expecting a harvest.

When you expect something, you prepare for the results. Remember: expectation = preparation. If you expect an A on an exam, you will prepare or study for the exam. On the other hand, if you don't expect an A, you won't prepare as much, and you will reap exactly what you expected to. There are times when we apply ourselves wholeheartedly and experience a lesser harvest than we expected, but with consistent and repeated positive action along with expectation, success will come. So, as you are continually expecting successful results, you should continue to prepare and expect. The law of sowing and reaping applies to all, whether we acknowledge it or not.

There is collective energy in our society that promotes getting something for nothing. Some choose to make excuses and expect success to be handed to them on a silver platter. But this concept goes against the very grain of having integrity and doesn't appeal to those who take pride in being productive and tapping into their talents to contribute to society.

We have been given everything we need to be productive, successful beings. It is up to each of us to find out where our success lies.

© Copyright by Lauri Williams 2009

Steps to Your Success; Not Only About You
Success is not solely about you. As you take action and pursue your success quest, resolve that your manifested success will

be about more than just you and fulfilling your own plans and desires. Resolve that it will instead possess a higher purpose.

More important, you are an instrument in the plan, so when embracing your success journey, you must maintain an open mind to receive guided instructions for your life. The answers are all around and, most important, within. Somewhere along the way, you may hear your vocation calling you. The word vocation is Latin for "calling," which comes from the word "voice."

What is your vocation saying, or what does it sound like? It may be a distinct feeling within your inner being. It may be a burst of light in the form of knowledge or zeal to take on a particular project. Tap into that power and discover your purpose to serve and to reach that level of success for you and for others. As you practice this, think of life as yarn and the effect of it unraveling.

What keeps you from unraveling your yarn? Perhaps it's our egos or our distorted view of ourselves because it prevents us from seeing past ourselves. Or in other words, we are eliminating great opportunities (EGO).

This is a problem for some, but we all know that every problem has a solution. Devise a strategy or plan to put your EGO to good use. EGO can work for you and not against you if you cleverly work your plan for success. How? Don't let it consume you.

Providing a service, product, skills, or talents for the betterment of mankind is the formula for success. In other words consider this equation: (ME + YOU = SUCCESS). It deflates the inflated EGO that eliminates great opportunity. Thus, creating an atmosphere where complete and increased success takes the reins and propels you further than you can imagine. However, there is one important ingredient—*YOU MUST BELIEVE IN YOU!*

Secure Your Destiny; Create Success
Every element incorporated within this book, if applied, can help to propel one closer to their God-given destiny. Many have utilized certain if not all aspects from this book and achieved success; so can you. I encourage you to study the record of others who have made it their mission in life to achieve their goals and secure their destiny in life; you will find that they understood the importance of looking past setbacks or limited thinking and focused on the importance of taking action and making better choices.

When you take the time to explore every possible area in your life, you will find that options or choices are all around you. You will see that you have opportunities to change your life for good and to contribute in making a better world. The choice is yours.

Choose to explore your options and not to limit them. You possess the power to shape your life moment by moment instead of being trapped by the "have to" syndrome. Often, we are placed in positions to do for others because we believe we "have to" do them?

In essence, you are programming your mind to believe that you have no options in saying no, not now, or this doesn't work for me.

Take, for example, the telephone. Nothing seems as urgent as a ringing telephone. There can be 10 customers in line at a store—people who made the effort to be there and are ready to make purchases—and the clerk will make them wait to answer a phone call from someone who hasn't even left their home. But do we really have to answer that phone? The caller is interrupting your day. He or she wants something from you—at least your time and maybe much more; whether or not you fulfill that request is up to you.

So the next time you think "I have to do this" or "I have to do that," stop and make yourself aware of this limiting thought. And then ask yourself: Do I really have to? Or do I have a choice—a better choice? It may take time for this new mindset to take effect, and for you to be comfortable doing it, but if you get into the habit of making conscious choices, then you are on the road to deprogramming those hindering and restricting thoughts from your life.

Exercise Your "Choice" Activity

Practice the following exercise for at least one month every time you think you have to do something, and you will discover you have more options than you thought you had.

1. **Pause.** Do you really have to do this? Decide not to act for five minutes.

2. **Examine Your Choices.** Instead, use your inner success powers to create as many choices as you can in five minutes. Be creative. I bet you score high.

3. **Enjoy Exploring Your Choices.** The more you perform this exercise, the more fun you will have learning to explore more ways for making decisions.

Do these exercises every day, and it will help you explore options that will change your life. You will find that you have tapped into your success powers (energies) that empower you to take control of your life and attain those things you desire.

APPENDIX

Keys to Releasing Your Success— God's Word

1. Joshua 1:1–9 KJV

2. Psalm 35:27 KJV

3. Deuteronomy 8:18 KJV

4. Psalm 37:5 KJV

5. Proverbs 16:3 KJV

6. Proverbs 11:14 KJV

7. Proverbs 24:16–18 KJV

8. Proverbs 27:17 KJV

9. James 1:3–4 KJV

10. Luke 18:1–8 KJV

11. Luke 6:38 KJV

12. Proverbs 2:1–9 KJV

13. Proverbs 4:23 KJV

14. Proverbs 6:6 KJV

15. Matthew 6:6 KJV

16. Matthew 6:33 KJV

Success Nuggets

- Success rewards you when you find it.
- Your love for yourself determines the level of success you want in your life.
- Success gives us choices. Meditate upon your success. Plan your life's course. What will it be?
- Opening your heart and mind to the unlimited success within you is like searching fervently for your glasses and realizing they were on your face all along.
- Success is built on *your* words.

- Success comes in various forms and only as fast as *you* allow it.
- EGO eliminates great opportunities for creating abundant success in your life. Deflate it, and you will go far.
- Success can be diminished. Success can be a talent seldom used. You choose it or lose it.
- Success is your genetic make-up. It is up to you to decide how you will live your life.
- Success is like a mirror. It is staring you in the face.
- Successful people are focused people. Focused people are successful people. Staying focused manifests your success quickly.
- You are CREATOR of your success world. You create your success outcome. It has nothing to do with chance or luck.
- Sow success. Reap success. Go! Be successful and increase!
- To forgive means you are creating room for your success to shine through YOU.
- Success is when you know your PURPOSE.
- The cause of diminished success is no action, no desire.
- Success is what *you* think.
- The remedy for an undesirable harvest in your life: When you change negative thoughts, you change the negative course of your life. Thus, if a negative person changes his or her thoughts, negative and unproductive people will eventually disappear.
- Success does not make you. YOU make success.

ABOUT THE AUTHOR

Lauri **Williams, CIEC, MCD, CEIP,** and Lay Chaplain is an author, military combat veteran, speaker, and entrepreneur coach with expertise in helping others with their career and Life goals. Lauri owns Always Making Your Mark LLC, based in North Little Rock, Arkansas. Lauri holds a bachelor's degree in human services, and a master's degree in human resources management, and she serves as Lay Chaplain for Community of Hope International (COHI).

Lauri has published several books, including: *Six Steps Six Figures: A Power-Packed Guide for Your Career Goals and Life God's Way* (first edition). Lauri coauthored the powerful *Stepping Stones to Success* with renowned authors Jack Canfield (*Chicken Soup for the Soul*), Deepak Chopra, and Dennis Waitley (*The Secret*). She also coauthored *Life Is an Attitude: The Power of Positive Living* (Professional Women's Network).

Lauri Williams has been interviewed by various media outlets including the *US News and World Report*, *Ebony*

Magazine, Creators Syndicate, and Los Angeles Community Voices. Lauri has a passion for poetry. She published her poem, "Breath Taking," in The Literary Magazine by the University of Maryland Asian Division. "Who Do You Say I AM" was published in "Echoes of Yesterday" by The National Library of Poetry.

How to Reach the Author:
I would love to hear from you. Read amazing testimonies you have on *Six Steps Six Figures, A Power-Packed Guide For Your Career Goals & Life God's Way*, 2nd Edition Updated and Expanded, or submit your own story of your experience employing strategic elements within this book.

Write me: Lauri Williams, CIEC, MCD, CEIP,
Lay Chaplain

Always Making Your Mark LLC
P.O. Box 94797
North Little Rock, AR 72190
(501) 240-3491

*I hope you enjoyed this book.
Would you do me a favor?*

I would love to hear from you and read amazing testimonies you have or submit your own story of your experience employing strategic elements within this book. Your opinion is invaluable. Would you take a few moments now to share your assessment of my book on any book review website you prefer? Your opinion will help the book marketplace become more transparent and useful to all.

Thank you very much!

www.ingramcontent.com/pod-product-compliance
Lightning Source LLC
Chambersburg PA
CBHW071346080526
44587CB00017B/2980